THE
MAGICAL & RITUAL
USE OF
HERBS

By the same author:
THE MAGICAL & RITUAL USE OF APHRODISIACS

THE
MAGICAL & RITUAL
USE OF
HERBS

RICHARD ALAN MILLER

DESTINY BOOKS
New York

Destiny Books
377 Park Avenue South
New York, NY 10016

Special thanks to Kirk Bergman (Frater 250).

I wish to dedicate this book to Michael Lafferty and Nancy
Hartzog for the use of their fantasy.

Library of Congress Cataloging in Publication Data.

Miller, Richard Alan, 1931-
   The magical and ritual use of herbs.
   Bibliography: p.
   Includes indexes.
   1. Psychotropic plants — Folklore. 2. Psychotropic
plants. I. Title.
GR790.P45M54 1983   615'.78   83-7457
ISBN 0-89281-047-5

Destiny Books is a division of Inner Traditions International

Printed in the United States

10 9 8 7 6 5 4

"Merlin put it very succinctly to Arthur in a book by T. H. White: 'Anything not specifically forbidden is mandatory'."

The Omega Principal

Contents

Introduction

PURPOSE

*To provide the explorer with concise
information on various legal psychotropic
botanicals now available.*

ORIENTATION

*To provide ritual use of these legal
mind altering sacraments.*

Ritual indicates the need in man to break the
barriers of the ego in order to become a part of something
greater. Ritual can be seen as the outward expression or
visible form of an inward or spiritual grace that is occurring. Rites are calculated to arouse the sentiments that
support a given pathworking or goal. The value of ritual:

(a) It is a method of organizing an experience.
     The manner in which the experience is
     "perceived" will determine the possible ways
     the experience might be used. This allows
     more conscious control of our growth and
     development.

(b) It lends grace and style to action. This
     prevents clumsy uncertainty, wasted energy
     and distractions.

(c) It helps the general atmosphere by using
     specific symbolism.

These are necessary to conjure a frame of mind conducive to the experience desired.

In psychology, ritual is often considered the celebration of a Myth. The construct of the ritual can be seen as the enactment of this Myth, as Myth would be represented as the source. Ritual is a projection of this Myth.

Since ritual is the externalization of something internal, Myth has a more archetypal* rather than logical structure to it. Rituals reveal values at their most fundamental level. Man expresses in ritual what moves him most.

Therefore: *The symbol always originates on the inside and is projected outward.*

Ceremonials and rituals are the means provided by society for periodically drawing up the sums of energy attached to the symbols. As symbols sink back into the unconscious, the ritual is a technique for bringing the symbols back out into a more common awareness.

Magick has been defined as "the Science and Art of causing changes to occur in conformity with Will". This is a philosophical concept which states that conflict only occurs when one is not living their true Will. The purpose or goal in Magick, then, is to discover that true Will (not necessarily desire) and then live It.

Therefore: *Every intential act is a Magickal Act.*

Whenever an individual changes their perception of reality, they also change the possible ways that reality can affect them. This is linked with attitudes, expectations and projections.

Therefore: *Whenever an individual takes a mind alterant, they are [by definition] performing an Act of Magick.*

Rituals can thus be used to "program" a religious

---

*"....the archetypes, as structural forming elements in the unconscious give rise both to the fantasy lives in individual children and to the mythologies of a people."　　　　　　　　　**C.G. Jung**

awakening, an awareness of something more spiritual than just the physical world. The Art of Magick is to blend Science with ritual. In this case, a thorough study of the chemistry of each herb is examined to determine how it will affect conscious perception of reality. With this information, the individual is then capable of controlling that experience, thus allowing more control of who they become....

Some of the materials discussed are quite dangerous and there are notes of caution. They are included because many people have already shown interest in experimenting with them. I feel that it is important to discuss these botanicals, meanwhile clearly indicating their potential dangers.

Although I am confident in the accuracy of this information, I can in no way assume responsibility for the experiences of persons following these traditions for personal drug use.

When experimenting with unfamiliar substances it is wise to use very small portions at first. The biochemistry of one person may be different from that of another. Some individuals are allergic* to substances upon which others thrive. Also, one's body needs may vary at different times. If there are any undesirable effects it is not advisable to continue use of that substance.

If there are no effects, desirable or undesirable, gradually and cautiously increase the quantity of the sacrament. Experimentation is absolutely where it is at. Spirituality does not lie in what you are doing, but rather, how you do it. There is no greater reflection of true Will than personal experience. *Do what thou wilt shall be the whole of the Law.*

---

*An allergic study can be made by scratching the skin with a sterilized pin and a sample of the herb considered. The scratches should be one-half inch long and not draw blood. If the scratch from the herb creates an undesired irritation within 60 minutes, you are most likely to have an undesired effect using this herb.

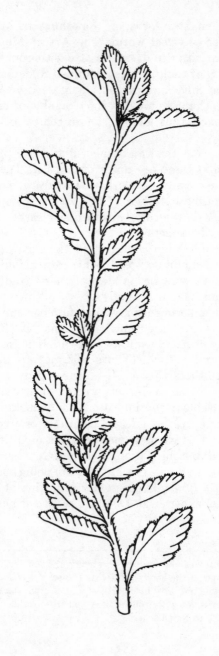

A sacrament to improve
and tone sexuality

Damiana

Family: Turneraceae.

Botanical Name: *Turnera diffusa.*

Synonyms: Mexican Damiana.

Geographical Location: Tropical parts of the Americas, particularly Texas and Mexico. It is also harvested in Africa.

Habitat: Grows in dry soil. Needs the sun. A desert is perfect.

Botanical Description: A small shrub with ovate leaves that are broadest toward the top end. The leaves are smooth and pale green on the upper side and smooth on the undersides except for a few hairs on the ribs. The flowers are yellow, arising singly from axila of the leaves followed by a one-celled capsule splitting into three pieces. The flower has an aromatic smell with a bitterish taste.

History

Many women in Mexico have found that a cup of damiana tea taken one hour or two before intercourse helps them to get really immersed in the sex act. It is believed to have a tonic affect upon the sexual organs and the nervous system. Most effective when used in combination with saw palmetto berries (Serenoa repens) in a 1:1 ratio.

Chemistry

Undetermined principle in oily fraction of extract.

Primary Effects

Mild aphrodisiac and marijuana-like euphoria, lasts about 1½ hours.

Preparation

In the book, *A Manual of Sex Magick*, Louis J. Culling describes a drink prepared by taking two heaping tablespoons of dried damiana leaves and boiling them in one cup of water for 5 minutes. It is allowed to cool, strained and drunk in the evening. He recommends continued use for a two week period for significant results.

Ritual Use

This is a fine recipe for making an aphrodisiacal cordial of damiana:

a) Soak 1 ounce damiana leaves in 1 pint of vodka for five days.
b) Pour off the liquid, strain and filter through a conical coffee filter paper.
c) Soak remaining alcohol-drenched leaves in ¾ pint distilled or spring water for another five days.
d) Pour off the liquids, strain and filter as before.
e) Warm water extracts to 160 °F. and dissolve ½-1 cup of honey.
f) Combine alcoholic and aqueous extractions. Age for one month. During the aging a sediment will form as the liqueur clarifies. The sediment is harmless but you may wish to siphon the clear liqueur from it.

g) One or two cordial glasses of the beverage may be taken nightly for the best results...It tastes exquisite.

Small quantities of liqueur are excellent for any ritual oriented toward Sex Magick. Although the chemistry is unknown, it is true that both tradition and lineage play an extensive role in the atmosphere and mode. I therefore recommend that damiana be used as a sacrament to improve and tone sexuality.

Note of Caution: *Excessive long-term use may be toxic to the liver. Although this is unconfirmed, those evening cordials will....*

It can make a really fine smoke if used in a waterpipe. A recommended blend for a "marijuana-like" high is:

> 4 parts damiana leaf
> 4 parts scullcap herb
> ½ part lobelia herb
> 4 parts passion flower herb
> 1 part spearmint leaf

This blend is now known as Yuba Gold.

*A sacrament for the ritual
greeting smoke [a marijuana substitute]*

Passion Flower

Family: Passifloraceae (Passion-flower family).

Botanical Name: *Passiflora Incarnata.*

Synonyms: None given.

Geographical Location: Native from Virginia, south and west to Florida and Texas, West Indies. Now cultivated throughout the world.

Habitat: Light rich soil which is dry.

Botanical Description: This herb has a perennial root that bears hairy climbing vines. The leaves have three to five lobes with finely serrated edges and solitary white flowers containing a purple, blue, or pink crown in the center. The fruit when ripe is oval shaped and orange colored called a maypop. The maypop berry contains many seeds and the yellow inside pulp is sweet and edible.

History

The Catholics, when the plant was first introduced in Europe, saw it as a symbolic representation of the "Passion of Christ." The corona was the crown of thorns; the 5 sepals and 5 petals symbolized the 10 Apostles. The other parts of the flower represented the nails and the wounds. The symbolism is the key to its use. It links the correspondences and creates a literal reality—through the construction of an archetype.

Chemistry

Harmine and related alkaloids. Called a psychic sedative. Isomer harmaline has been tried in Parkinsonism. It is a very potent MAO inhibitor. (See footnote page 88).

Harmine

Primary Effects

When smoked, very mild, short-lasting marijuana high. It acts both as a sedative and a tranquilizer. In larger quantities, it acts more as a hallucinogen.

Preparation

Usually smoked in combination with damiana, scullcap, and peppermint (for flavor). (See footnote page 17).

Ritual Use

Alchemy has a number of interesting "faces." In regards to symbolism, various elements are classified into a system of qualities. By appropriately mixing these qualities, new elements are created.

An example would be that of combining the heat of fire with the wetness of water, thus creating air which is hot and wet. A more contemporary example would be that "although the person had never lectured before, he was excellent because he had the qualities of enthusiasm and knowledge about the subject." The imagination is one of the great pointers to reality. It is the creative part which enables us to survive and "progress." By taking imagination seriously, beyond the level of mere personal fantasy, it tends to structure itself to major archetypal patterns.

Synchronicity is the key. By using tables of correspondences (Liber 777, for example) to project and create the archetype, a literal reality is created. We should not separate our sciences and technologies from a religious context.

The extraction of alkaloids can be seen as an alchemical process. Use ethyl alcohol or any drinking alcohol. The yield is approximately 1 gm of mixed harmal alkaloids per kilo of herb. That's a lot of hits...(and symbolism).

Note of Caution: *Harmala alkaloids are potent MAO inhibitors. [See Yohimbe* Note of Caution *page 88*].

Excellent as a tea to rid headaches and insomnia.

Betel Nut

Family: Palmaceau (Palm family).

Botanical Name: *Aveca catechu.*

Synonyms: areca nut, pinang, siri, supari (Hindu), and ping lang (Chinese).

Geographical Location: India, Malay and Polynesia.

Habitat: Grows everywhere on South Pacific Islands.

Botanical Description: A slender climbing tree up to 75 feet high, with ringed trunk that is usually trained on poles or trellis in a hot but shady environment. The leaf blades grow to be as much as three feet across with many pinnae; that is, a compound leaf with many divisions separated by veins.

History

In 1930 it was estimated that there were at least 20,000,000 betel chewers in India. Betel palms produce about 250 seeds or nuts per year and millions of these trees are under cultivation. It is one of the world's most popular plants, with the leaf being used as a paper for rolling tobaccos and herbs (yet few Western people have ever heard of it). The regular use of betel nut does, in time, stain the mouth, gums, and teeth a deep red. Asian betel chewers, however, are quite proud of these stains.

Chemistry

Arecoline, a volatile oil, is released from the nut by saliva and lime (Calcium oxide). Betel leaf contains chavicol, allylpyrocathechol, chavibetol and cadinene.

Arecoline

Arecoline is in the same cholinergic alkaloids group as muscarine, found in the divine mushroom, Soma (Fly Agaric, page 90).

Primary Effects

Arecoline—mild CNS (Central Nervous System) stimulant. It increases respiration, decreases work load of the heart.

Preparation

Mix ½ gm of burnt lime (hydrated calcium oxide) with one betel nut, preferably in a semi-powdered form. Place in the side of the mouth like a plug of tobacco for a two hour period, and spit the saliva occasionally.

Because of the primary effects of arecoline, betel nut is well suited for labor. The CNS stimulant allows a journey to become more "vivid" simply by allowing time to be perceived differently. The herb is perfect for weekend journeys to friends in the country, or for ceremonial work on your land.

Ritual Use

The Malayan technique for using betel nut is to mix a mash or powdered betel nut, some catechu gum from the Malayan acacia tree (Acacia catechu), a pinch of burnt lime, and a dash of nutmeg, cardamon or tumeric for flavor. This mash is then rolled up in a leaf from the betel vine (Piper chavica betel).

These betel morsels are sold on the streets or markets as candy (with no current government control).

Note of Caution: *Excessive arecoline from either over use or chewing unripe areca nuts, which contain larger quantities of the oil, can cause innebriation, dizziness, and diarrhea. Also, causes damages to the teeth and soft tissue of the mouth with prolonged useage.*

Betel nut is considered an aphrodesiac because it stimulates one's available energy and elevates moods rather than directly influencing sexual organs. It is currently used like coffee [*brewed*] or cigarettes [*mint bidis*] in this country.

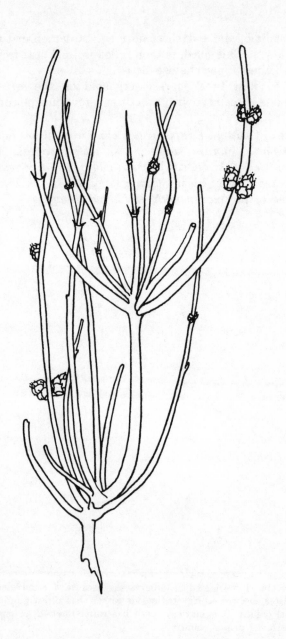

A stimulant sacrament
to improve breathing

Mormon Tea

Family: Gnetaceae.

Botanical Name: *Ephedra nevadensis.*

Synonyms: stick tea, desert tea, squaw tea, brigham weed, teamsters tea, and popotillo.

Geographical Location: American southwest. The variety *Ephedra vulgaris* is found in West Central China, Southern Siberia and Japan.

Habitat: Sandy seashores or temperate climates of both hemispheres.

Botanical Description: The herb has both male and female flowers. The males containing stamins are found together on catkins while the females containing pistils arising from a two-leaved flower branch that is supported on axillary stalks coming from the stems. The fruit consists of two pistil-like capsules containing a juicy cone-shaped seed in each capsule. The stems or branches are slender and erect with small leaves somewhat like scales on the stem.

History

Chinese ephedra has been used medicinally for more than 5,000 years. In 2,700 B.C., Shen Mung, the father of Chinese medicine used the dried roots and stems as a decongestant to treat coughs, colds, headaches, and fever. Its Chinese name is *Ma Huang*.

Some species of ephedra were made into a fermented drink and used ceremonially by Vedic and Zoroastrian priests for tantric lunar rites.

Chemistry

Mormon tea contains ephedrine, D-norpseudo-ephedrine and tannin. Ephedrine exhibits most of the effects of sympathetic stimulation.

Ephedrine Sulfate (Ma Huang)

Ma Huang has 4× the effect of ephedrine to mormon tea because pseudoephedrine has less vascular action but maintained bronchial effect. They both cost the same per pound.

Primary Effects

Powerful decongestant. Stimulant, blood pressure may rise moderately, heart rate and cardiac output increased. Bronchi are relaxed and dilated.

Preparation

The Chinese technique is to bring a large pan of water to boil. Put one to two ounces of mormon tea (or ephedra) into the boiling water and put a lid on. Allow to boil for 5 minutes then turn down. Three to four cups of the liquid should "get you off"...

Ritual Use

The breath is considered the original source of life in China. Any herb which improved breathing was considered a sacrament. A simple ritual used today involves the use of Ma Huang and Tiger Balm (an ointment containing camphor).

If the herb is left on the stove for several days, fermentation occurs. The water is usually brought to a boil at least once each day. After the fourth day, the brew becomes quite strong as a stimulant. Breathing is improved by placing Tiger Balm on the lip under the nose and inhaling the fumes of ephedra. After five minutes of this, drink three to four cups of the liquid. The resultant increase in energy will be seen to directly relate to the ease in breathing.

Note of Caution: *If used in excess [i.e. every day for the next three weeks], there is the possibility of losing elasticity in the blood vessels and bronchial tubes. Also, ephedra will produce vertigo, nervousness, and insomnia with prolonged use. It should not be used if one suffers from high blood pressure, heart disease, diabetes, or thyroid problems.*

Ephedrine is used extensively in asthma to produce continued bronchial dilation. Ephenepherine and Emperin codeine contain ephedrine as the principle activant.

Guarana

Family: Sapindaceae (Soapberry family).

Botanical Name: *Paullinia cupana.*

Synonyms: Panela supana, Brazilian cocoa, Uabano.

Geographical Location: South America, particularly north and west Brazil and in Venezuela.

Habitat: South American tropical jungles, Amazon.

Botanical Description: A climbing shrub with divided compound leaves. The flowers are yellow in an open cluster. The three-celled capsuled fruit contains a seed resembling small horse chestnuts in each of the three cells. The fresh seeds are flesh colored and are easily separated from the fruit after drying. The seeds are washing and roasted for six hours in preparation for use.

History

Many of our weight problems in the U.S. stem from our diet and awarness of eating habits and patterns. An example would be our tradition of having three meals each day. The origin of this myth is Chinese.

The Chinese have an ancient legend which states that once God requested the Ox-god to tell man he needed to eat only once every third day. The Ox-god was forgetful and accidentally told man he needed to eat three times each day...hence our myth of three meals per day!

This was nine times more food than man needed to eat, and there was no way he could produce that quantity of food. As punishment, God made the Ox-god a beast of burden, to serve man and help produce that quantity of food.... The Ox is now considered "sacred" in most of the Eastern countries. After all, he is a god.

In his novel *Moonchild*, Aleister Crowley shows the very little difference, barring our Occidental subtlety, between the above Chinese philosophy and the English:

"The Chinese bury a man alive in an ant heap;
the English introduce him to a woman."

Diet and food consciousness have become so important today that dieting has taken an air of the ceremonial. Vanity is ALL and tradition prevails...

Guarana was first used by the Quaramis, a tribe of South American Indians, for bowel complaints. It was also used by Brazilian miners as a preventative for their many diseases, but mainly as a refreshing beverage. Guarana also is a main ingredient in a favorite diet beverage in Brazil.

Chemistry

Guarana falls in the methylated purine group containing 5% caffeine, three times as much as in normal coffee. Guarana is considered the strongest naturally

Caffeine

occuring methylxanthines. It has the same chemical composition as caffeine, theine and cocaine, and the same physiological action.

Other methylated purines are:

a) Coffee. From *Coffea arabica*, an Arabian bush; bean contains 1%-2% caffeine.

b) Tea. From *Camelia theca*, an Asian bush; leaves contain 2%-4% caffeine, and theobromine and theophylline.

c) Cacao. From *Theobroma cacao*, Aztec, chocolate; beans contain about 2% theobromine and traces of caffeine and theophylline.

d) Mate . From *Ilex paraguyensis*, a South American bush; leaves contain 2½% caffeine.

e) Kola. From *Cola nitida*, an African nut; contains 3% caffeine.

Primary Effects

Stimulant. Quickens perceptions, wakefulness, slows the pulse, impairs the appetite and can be used for long drives or long work hours. "Speed".

Preparation

Powder guarana seed with a mortar and pestle or coffee grinder. Prepare like coffee using the grinds several times. Two nuts are recommended per cup. (The seed should crush between finger and thumb). The powder can also be capped.

Ritual Use

The seed was gathered usually in October, ground, and then mixed with cassava flour, made into a paste with water and dried in the sun. The paste was often shaped into sticks dried over fires. As an energy source or stimulant, there is none better. It also impairs the appetite.

MATE'

In many traditions, your physical body is considered your temple. It is a direct mirror of the state of your mind. It reflects directly whether you are a happy person or not.

Fasting has been considered to be one of the finest disciplines in uniting the mind and body in most societies. Guarana can be used as a training sacrament for achieving a conscious control over the physical body through the technique of fasting.

Consider the following schedule as an exercise:

1) First month, fast one day per week, arbitrarily chosen but adhered to rigorously. This means no food, only water or tea (with guarana). Keep a log on psychological outlook.
2) Second month, fast two days, not consecutively, each week.
3) Third month, add a third day of fasting every other week. Observe change in your own psychology. Develop your own schedule. Also note the tone in your temple!

Using the caffeine speeds up metabolism and kills the appetite. It can be used as a sacrament to aid the fast.

Note of Caution: *Long-term or excessive use alters the bloodsugar. This will cause nervousness, insomnia, and possible psychic habituation.*

Guarana can also be used as a tonic nervine against hangovers, menstrual-type headaches and neuralgia.

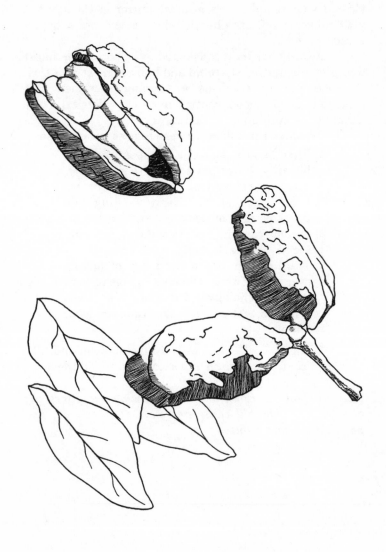

*A sacrament to stimulate sexual energies
and to combat fatigue*

Kola Nut

Family: Sterculiaceae (Cacao family).

Botanical Name: *Cola nitida.*

Synonyms: Cola.

Geographical Location: Native to West Africa, particularly North Ashanti and Sierra Leone.

Habitat: Near river beds of tropical jungles.

Botanical Description: A tree growing from forty to sixty feet high that has leaves six to eight inches long pointed at both ends. It has yellow flowers spotted with purple. The fruit is yellowish-brown divided into five segments in which one to three of these segments contain seeds. The seeds are flat in shape and are one and one-half inches long.

History

This was the one-time ingredient in Coca Cola after cocaine became illegal. Today, even kola nut is not used in this "great American drink". It is still used as a drink in Jamaica and Brazil, its primary attribute being a sexual stimulant similar to cocaine.

The powdered seeds are extensively used as a condiment by the natives of Africa, West Indies and

Brazil. A small piece of seed is chewed before meals to promote digestion and to improve the flavor of anything eaten after it. The powder was applied to cuts.

Chemistry

Contains 3% caffeine, theobromine, and kolanin (a glucoside). Also contains some tannin and starch. Caffeine stimulates all parts of the CNS, especially the cerebral cortex and medullary center. Kolanin (a

Caffeine

Theobromine

glucoside) is a source for carbohydrates, the "fuel" needed for the body's energy. This combination aids the combustion of fats and carbohydrates. It also reduces combustion of nitrogen and phosphorus in the body.

Primary Effects

Stimulates and economizes muscular and nervous energies. Considered a strong stimulant.

Preparation

One tablespoon of kola nut powder into a cup of black coffee is the recommended way of ingestion. You might add some honey. It is quite chalky. Another technique is to cap the powder in '00' caps. However, the oils do not hit the stomach in the same manner and is only used this way because of its chalk-like taste.

Ritual Use

Most of the original concepts of sex, as it relates to Magic, were from the earlier Hindu traditions of Tantra. They believed sex contained an energy which could change the physical world. The psychological implications are covered in the ritual use section of psilocybe mushrooms. (page 14).

This psycho-sexual energy is the principle element behind contemporary western Magick today. It is the single, strongest emotion-alterant available which can be disciplined. It is the foundation of tantra. A path to the use of this psyco-sexual power begins with a recognition and then overcoming of restrictive sexual prejudices. The first place to start is to cultivate intense gonadal awareness through the conscious tightening of the pelvic region. There are a series of exercises where this is accomplished by deliberate, selected contraction-and-relaxation of the anal and urethral (or urinary) muscles.

Two suggested exercises in *Sexual Occultism* by John Mumford given have been used as a tantric yoga tradition for thousands of years in India and the Middle East. These particular exercises may be used as a ritual to highten orgasms:

EXERCISE ONE: To control ejaculation
and orgasm (MOOLA BANDHA)

This exercise is a pelvic contraction lock which begins at the anal muscles and spreads forward to the genitals. The correct feeling of this anal lock is like the sensation you feel when you retain an enema (hold back the passage of stool from the bowel). The method:

1) Sit erect in a comfortable position, hands palm-up on thighs.
2) Focus attention on anal region. Begin with awareness of chair exerting pressure up against the behind. Pinpoint consciousness to anus.
3) Inhale one-half lungful of air, swallow and hold breath.
4) Slowly contract the anus while holding breath. Continue to hold breath.
5) Women should spread their pelvic region

forward from the anus, until a distinct twitch is felt in the vaginal lips. Men should spread their pelvic region forward from the anus until a distinct pull is felt on the testicle.

6) Now release pelvic contraction totally. Inhale and then exhale fully.

The advantages of this exercise are:

a) In women, it tightens slack vaginal walls. In men, it reduces tendency for premature ejaculation.

b) It sends a blood flush to the uro-genital system.

c) It tones anal muscles. This prevents and even cures hemorrhoids and other anal purities.

d) It awakens the Mooladahara Chakra.

EXERCISE TWO: To increase exectile potency and clitoral sensitivity.
(VAJROLI MUDRA)

This exercise involves the urethral sphincter closure, exactly as when you cut off the flow of urine in midstream while voiding. For a preliminary step to prepare for this exercise, drink several pints of water or beer on an empty stomach. In one hour empty the bladder. As you do, practice cutting off and restraining the urine flow at least one dozen times while the bladder drains. The method:

1) Sit erect in a comfortable position, hands palm-up on thighs.

2) Focus attention on urethral sphincter. This is below the clitoris for women and at the base of the penis in men.

3) Inhale one-half lungful of air, swallow and hold breath.

4) Contract urethral orifice exactly as if cutting off urine flow as in the preliminary

exercise. At the same time pull up on lower abdomen, as if attempting to suck your genitals into the pelvis. Relax contraction and repeat as many times as possible while holding your breath. Allow sexual excitement to occur.

5) Cease contractions, relax abdomen, inhale and then exhale fully.

For women to check to see if they are performing the exercise correctly, insert one or two fingers into vagina and perform the exercise (Vajroli Mudra). If it is done correctly, contractions should spread, causing the vagina to close on fingers.

In men, perform the exercise (Vajroli Mudra) naked in front of the mirror. Watch to see if head of penis twitches or elevates slightly with each contraction.

a) It increases clitoral sensitivity in women, and erectile potency in men.

b) It sends blood flush to uro-genital system.

c) It tones urethral sphincter. This cures urinary stress incontinence.

d) It awakens Swadhisthana Chakra.

Moola Banda should be followed by Vajroli Mudra daily starting with 10 each. You should add 5 per day each week until you are doing 60 of each per day.

These exercises develop pelvic thrust ability in males and pelvic gripping power in the females. This enhances sensitivity and control in both sexes during intercourse. May you never thirst.

Note of Caution: *Excessive use of caffeine over long periods can be debilitating to the sexual function. It may also cause nervousness, insomnia, habituation.*

Kola nut is classified as a nerve stimulant and true aphrodisiac. It can also be used to curb the appetite and lose weight.

*A sacrament used in the ritual
smoking blend, Yuba Gold*

Lobelia

Family: Lobeliaceae (or Campanulaceae family).

Botanical Name: *Lobelia inflata.*

Synonyms: Indian tobacco, Gagroot, Vomitroot, Bladderpod.

Geographic Location: All parts of the United States.

Habitat: Fields, woods and meadows.

Botanical Description: The herb is an annual indigenious to North America, found in pastures and cultivated fields. The erect, angular stem grows from six inches to three feet tall and is hairy with a milky sap. The leaves are thin and light green in an ovoid shape, hairy with blunt saw-like teeth on the edge. Numerous small blue flowers growing in spine-like pods arranged in succession at the top of the stem. The fruit is a two-celled oval capsule containing numerous small brown seeds.

History

In North America *lobelia* found its way into medicine in 1785. Cutler, in his published account of herbs, stated that when the leaves were chewed, they "produced giddiness and pain of the head, with trembling

43

agitation". The Penobscot Indians of eastern North America used it as a tobacco in the early nineteenth century. A similar species was smoked by the Mapuche Indians of Chile for the narcotic effect. They called the weed *tuba* or *tobaco del diablo*.

Chemistry

Active alkaloids are lobeline, lobelanidine and norlobelanidine. Although these constituents are not known to have hallucinogenic effects, d-lobeline is a carotid body stimulant.

$$HO-CH-CH_2-{\overset{\displaystyle \big|}{N}}-CH_2-CH-OH$$

$$CH_3$$
$$\circ \; \tfrac{1}{2} H_2SO_4$$

Lobeline Sulfate (Nikoban)

Primary Effects

When *very* small quantities are added to a cigarette and smoked, the effect is a mild marijuana-like euphoria. It acts simultaneously as a stimulant and a relaxant. Lesser amounts tend to act as a stimulant, larger amounts as a depressant. It alters the mental state.

Preparation

Only a pinch should be added to steeping tea, preferably peppermint and chamomile. By itself, it is *very* harsh.

Ritual Use

The social practice of setting a pipe for guests is fairly common, even today. The purpose is a sort of security where everyone sits and centers as a group. The sacrament has varied from generation to another. Within the American Indian tradition, the pipe bowl is always nearest the center of the circle, being passed from right to left. The host always loads the first bowl.

To make an excellent smoking blend, see footnote of Damiana (page 17).

Note of Caution: *Normal amounts may cause nausea, vomiting and circulatory disturbances.*

Lobelia is probably considered to be one of the best herbals used as an expectorant. Also excellent when there is a need to induce vomiting.

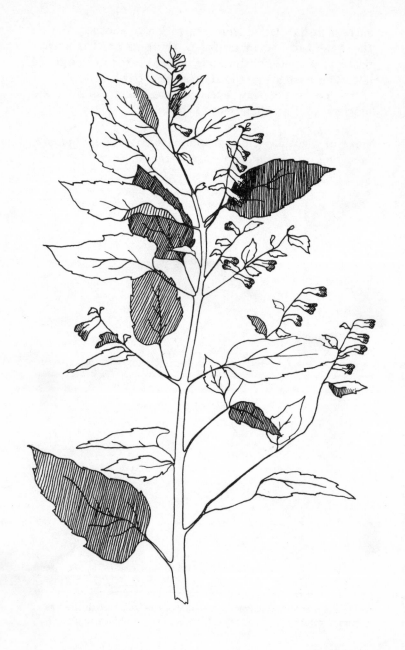

A sacrament for healing
the nerves

Scullcap

Family: (Mint family).

Botanical Name: *Scutellaria Lateriflora.*

Synonyms: Mad dogweed, blue Pimpernell, Hood-wort.

Geographical Location: East coast of America from Connecticut south to Florida and as far west as Texas. Europe.

Habitat: Indigenous herb, growing in damp places; meadows, ditches, and the side of ponds. Flowers in July and August.

Botanical Description: A perennial herb that has a big porous, yellow root stock which produces a branching stem growing from one to three feet in height. The leaves grow in opposite pairs up the stem and have saw-like points on the edges forming a point at the end. The flowers grow from axils at the stem and are two lipped; pale purple or blue in color.

History

Ancient herbalists named it scullcap because its blossoms resembled the human skull. It has also been known as Mad dogweed and Madweed because it cured hydrophobia. The herbalists' guild for determining the use of an herb, like scullcap, was termed "the doctrine of signatures." They took into consideration the shape and color of the plant's leaves and flowers. These were signs as to what organs of the body respond to medicines prepared by these herbs:

a) Red is the color of the blood. It was concluded that plants bearing red flowers would act on the blood. As research now indicates, red-flowered plants are rich in iron for the hemoglobin of the blood. An example would be red clover.

b) Blue is a soothing sedative color. These types of plants are thus helpful to brain and nerves. Plants with blue flowers are rich in potassium and phosphorus, which are minerals that act on the brain and nerves. Examples are *scullcap, valerian* and *vervain.*

c) Yellow suggests bile; so herbs with yellow blossoms were given for digestive, liver and gall disorders. Yellow-flowered plants have an abundance of sodium, the mineral associated with digestion and liver secretions. Examples are *dandelion, celandine* and *barberry* (oregon grape); all with yellow roots, all proven remedies for stomach, liver, gall bladder and intestinal disorders.

Herbal literature describes *scullcap,* then, as being one of the finest nervines ever discovered.

Chemistry

None known.

Primary Effects

Scullcap is a great tranquilizer. If smoked, the effects are similar to marijuana. It is most soothing to mind and nerves and should be considered in all fear states, when there is mental confusion and inability to concentrate.

Preparation

Steep one ounce of scullcap in a pint of very hot water for twenty minutes. Drink three to four cups for most pronounced effects.

Ritual Use

Tantric yoga techniques have traditionally been used for self development using the male-female concept as a source of energy. There are a number of techniques in this system which can be used to physically heal such things as urinary infections and mental disorders. The ritual described in this section is a healing exercise which only works as well as the "visualization" required. Make no mistake, however; this exercise does work quite well:

a) Drink scullcap tea.

b) Face each other, male and female, naked and in a comfortable sitting position.

c) The woman sits with her hands in her lap. The male places his right hand on the top of her head, his left hand over her stomach.

d) The male then "visualizes" a large white ball of light originating over his head. This white ball then descends down into his head, through his right hand, down the female's body and out through his left hand. This "energy" is then visualized as circulating up his body, through his right hand and down her body again, forming a circular path of evergy.

e) The female "visualizes" this energy going down her body. She then directs it to the place which needs healing...this place is arbitrary, chosen before the ritual. When she "feels" the energy in that place, she chants **AUM**.

f) When the female is finished chanting, she then repeats the ritual, performing the part the male did. The male does not chant **AUM** until he "feels" more energy at his chosen site for healing than he gave her; when he does, he then chants **AUM**.

g) When the male is finished chanting, he repeats this ritual back to the female, again with her chanting **AUM only** when she "feels" more energy than she did the first time.

h) This ritual is continued 4-5 times until each fall back exhausted. You may make love at this time.

If this exercise is repeated each night for one week, the possibilities are perpetual potential. You can heal such things as flu, colds, urinary diseases and even upset minds. There is, however, more actually occurring than the "power of the mind"....

Note of Caution: *It is not recommended that scullcap be used in combination with any pharmaceutical tranquilizers. It is strong in itself and the chemistry has yet to be identified.*

Smaller doses are safe for children, to eliminate headaches or when fitful sleep is occurring.

Valerian Root

Family: Valerianaceae (Valerian family).

Botanical Name: *Valeriana officinalis.*

Synonyms: Valerian, vandal root.

Geographical Location: Northern Hemisphere, America, England and especially Europe.

Habitat: Warm temperate regions near stands of water. The sides of riverbanks and irrigated fields, dry pastures and sun.

Botanical Description: A perennial plant about two to four feet high with a yellow-brown, tuberous rootstock that arises to a hollow angular, furrowed stem with leaves growing in pairs that are pinnate, that is, feather-formed leaflets that are sharply toothed. The flowers are small and clustered together at the top of the stem and are rose colored to reddish, sometimes white in color.

History

The dried rhyzome and roots of this herb were historically used as a nerve sedative and antispasmodic, and a remedy for hysteria and other nervous complaints. It was also used for menstral periods, to heal inward sores and outward wounds. Boiled with licorice, raisin and anise seed, it was used as an expectorant for phlegm in difficult coughs and lung congestion.

Its odor is very unpleasant, smelling much like "dirty feet." Cats, however, find it preferable to catnip, and it can be stuffed into pillows for cats.

Chemistry

Chatinine and velerine alkaloids. These oils are very similar to those in valium.

Valium

The oils seem to excite the cerebro-spinal system... making them perfect for massage!

Primary Effects

Muscle relaxant and mild tranquilizer...as if floating in the air...

Preparation

Since the oils are volatile and evaporate into a vapor at fairly low temperatures, the root is generally placed in non-boiling water and allowed to steep for twenty minutes. Be sure to cover the pan so as to not allow the oils to evaporate into the air. Normal quantities are a tablespoon of valerian root per cup of water. This is approximately equivalent to a #10 Valium (10 mg).

Ritual Use

Massage is perhaps one of the single most important techniques for healing. The concept and visualization of "chi" is a valid model for manipulating the healing energies of the body. This "life-force" is thought to originate in the spine with its movement either going down the legs and out through the toes or up the back and along the arms, and then out through the fingers. In all techniques of massage using the visualization of chi, then, are some very basic, simple rules:

1) Once you begin to touch the body, the movement should always be away from the spine, either up the body and out through the fingers or down the legs and out through the toes. If you begin to massage the neck, then you must visualize and move that energy out through the arms and then the fingers. You should **not** make any movement down the back, in this case. The flow and direction of chi is very important.

2) Always keep contact with at least one of your hands on your partner's body (if you are reaching for oil, etc). Once you begin to touch the body, you should continue that movement until the energy is brought out through the feet or the hands.

3) Eventually your hands become tired and cramped. This is an "AMA explanation" for the energy cramp in your hands. In the Chinese system, however, it is believed that you have simply taken the nervous energy of your partner into your own aura. Their technique then is to shake their hands, snapping the excess nervous energy off into space. This model for visualizing the energy works. You relieve your cramps and the partner "feels" a definite loss of nervous energy.

4) The more you are able to visualize the movement of this energy, chi, the more real the experience of this massage is to your partner. They will literally feel the energy to the point of being really surprised!

5) Foot and ear massages are more important than neck and back massages. There are more meridian points in the ear than most of the rest of the body combined. It symbolizes the entire body in a fetal position. The foot also symbolizes the entire body as well and by learning Reflexology you can heal internal parts of the body by correct massage of the feet. Facial massages are always unexpected...

Note of Caution: *If you boil valerian root in water, you lose the oils and the only thing you have is a bad smell. Although the brew may smell bad, with the addition of peppermint/spearmint and honey, it does not taste bad at all. It can also be capped.*

Valerian can be served safely to small babies that are having trouble going to sleep. It is totally non-toxic. It relaxes their muscles and they can then fall asleep naturally. You should only use ¼ of a teaspoon to a cup of tea.

Wild Lettuce

Family: Compositae (Sunflower family).

Botanical Name: *Lactuca virosa.*

Synonyms: lettuce opium, lopium.

Geographical Location: Southern and Central Europe and the United States.

Habitat: Loose, rich, well-drained fields. Should be planted in late fall. Needs moisture.

Botanical Description: The herb is a biennial plant with a leafy, round stem that grows from two to seven feet high. The stem is erect and smooth, colored pale green and sometimes spotted with purple. The lower leaves are numerous and large, growing to be eighteen inches long. The upper stem leaves are small, scanty and grow alternately; clasping the stem with two small lobes. The heads are short stalked with numerous pale yellow flowers. The fruit is a rough black oval with a broad wing along the edge that narrows to a long white beak holding silvery tufts of hair.

History

Wild lettuce was traditionally dried and smoked like opium. It has also been used for nervousness and as a

59

sedative. It was considered milder than opium but just as "dreamy". Lettuce opium was often used by the North American Indians by smoking the dried resin or sap obtained from the plant. They cut the flower heads off, gathered the sap that drained off and then let it air dry. This process was done repeatedly over a two week period by cutting just a little bit off the top each time.

Chemistry

Active ingredient now identified as lactucarine (now known as lettuce opium. This contains 2% lactucin (similar structure to that of opium) plus lactucerol (also known as taraxasterol) and lactucic acid. Chemistry is not yet available on this new legal high. These ingredients appear in domestic lettuce as well, but less than one order of magnitude to wild lettuce.

Primary Effects

Mild narcotic and analgesic. Sedative which induces low alphoid activity rather than deep sleep. See Primary Effects section on Thorn Apple (page 123). Most dream states occur in REM (rapid eye movement) sleep, a state which is characterized by low alphoid activity.

Preparation

The easiest method is to dry the leaves and roots and smoke them in a large pipe. The general, commercial, technique, however, is to heat (not boil) the leaf in water for at least an 8 hour period. Then remove the liquid. Lactucarine goes into solution with water. A heat lamp is placed over the bowl of liquid and a fan is used to drive the water out of the extraction. The result will be a blackish gum which can be smoked best with a waterpipe and hot torch. The gum should be rolled in small balls and sealed in plastic to prevent them from drying out. The hotter the flame, the better the high.

A general amount for each person is approximately one ounce of wild lettuce or about ½ - 1 grams of the extract.

Ritual Use

The northern Indian schools of tantra have a popular internal cleansing method known as skank prakshalana. This ritual is particularly well-suited for the chemistry involved with opiates. The technique almost totally flushes out the gastro-intestinal tract by passing several gallons of saline solution from the mouth through the numerous convolutions of the intestinal tract and then out through the anus.

This passage and then expulsion of the fluid is assisted by special asanas (postures) which squeeze the stomach and wring out the gut. At initiation marijuana (bhang) or opium (lettuce opium could be used) is added to the Shank Prakshalana water. This produces the trance consciousness desired as the cleansing process deepens to levels other than the physical.

The Hopi Indian believes that these dream states contain more information about reality than the conscious waking state. Their emphasis is so great that dreams are recorded for their information content and discussed each day at breakfast for significance. Lettuce opium will enhance the vividness of dreams when smoked prior to sleep. You should keep a diary to review the contents at least once per week.

Note: some very important details will emerge which will be directly applicable to aid in the control of your conscious states and attitudes. The main function of dreams is to combine new or recent experiences with those from your past to create new attitudes. These new attitudes directly affect your future via projection and inhibition. They set up the limitations and possiblitiies available. Therefore, dreams, in one sense, can be seen as creating or causing the future.

One should spend more time on what we do when we "void-out" that one-third of our life....

"No one who does not know himself can
know others. And in each of us there is
another whom we do not know. He speaks

to us in dreams and tells us how differently he sees us from the way we see ourselves. When, therefore, we find ourselves in a different situation to which there is no solution, he can sometimes kindle a light that radically alters our attitude—the very attitude that led us into the difficult situation."

C. G. Jung

Note of Caution: *Homeopathic medicine recommends that anyone who suffers from any form of stomach disorders, especially ulcers, should not ingest any form of lettuce. This is due to the fact that all lettuces, even domestic, contain this lettuce opium product which will coat the stomach wall and reduce digestion processes. It also represses sex drives!*

A decoction of the leaf serves as an excellent face wash!

A sacrament for the liqueur
after a ritual

Wormwood

Family: Compositae (Sunflower or Aster family).

Botanical Name: *Artemisia absinthium.*

Synonyms: Absinth, green ginger.

Geographical Locations: All over the world, from the U.S. to Siberia.

Habitat: Roadsides, waste places and near the sea.

Botanical Description: The herb is a silky perennial plant supported by a woody rootstock producing many bushy stems that grow two to four feet in height. The stems are whitish covered closely with fine silk hairs. The leaves are hairy also, shaped with many blunt lobs of irregular symmetry. The flowers are small with globular heads of greenish-yellow color that are arranged on an erect leafy flower stem. The leaves and the flowers have a very bitter taste and characteristic odor.

History

The genus is named Artemisia from Artemis, the Greek name for Diana, Goddess of the Moon. In an early translation of the Herbarium of Apuleius:

"Of these worts that we name artemisia, it is said that Diana did find them and delivered their powers and leechdom to Chiron the Centaur, who first from these worts set forth a leechdom, and he named these worts from the name of Diana, Artemis, that is Artemisias."

Chemistry

Absinthine (a dimeric guaranolide) is the principle agent, anabsinthin and thiyone (a volatile oil) are also present. Absinthine is listed as a narcotic analgesic in the same group as codeine and dextromethorphan hydrobromide (Romilar).

Primary Effects

Narcotic-analgesic. It depresses the central medullary part of the brain, the area concerned with pain and anxiety.

Preparation

The herb is either smoked or prepared as a liqueur. The absinthine can be extracted with alcohol and water.

Ritual Use

An excellent liqueur can be made by taking one ounce of wormwood (preferably the flowers) and put them into a pint of brandy and let stand for six weeks. The resultant tincture is then combined with Pernod or anisette to make the classical absinthe. This is excellent for an after-dinner liqueur, or after a ritual where everyone is emotionally tired.

Note of Caution: *Excessive long-term use of liqueur may be habit-forming and debilitating. Ingestion of the above volatile oils as a tincture may cause gastro-intestinal disturbances and convulsions due to the thiyone.*

*A stimulant sacrament, used as a
tonic for alleviating fatigue.*

Calamus

Family: Araceae (Arum family).

Botanical Name: *Acorus Calamus.*

Synonyms: Sweet sedge, sweet flag, rat root, sweet myrtle, beewort, bachh (Hindu), racha (Vedic), shih-ch'ang pu (Chinese).

Geographical Location: Europe, Asia, China and North America from Nova Scotia to Minnesota, southward to Florida and Texas.

Habitat: Marshes, borders of streams and ponds. Commonly seen among cat-tails and other species of flag.

Botanical Description: A perennial herb somewhat resembling the iris that has a horizontal, creeping root-stock. It may grow to be five feet long. It can be distinguished from real iris by the Peculiar crimped edges of its leaves and their aromatic odor when bruised. The leaves are sword-like and grow from two to six feet high and a similar ridged flower stalk appears from the base of the outer leaves, and bears a cylindrical blunt spike or spadix covered by minute greenish-yellow flowers.

History

For over 2,000 years, calamus has been used by both the Moso sorcerers of Yunnan, China and the

Ayurvedic systems of medicine as a remedy for bronchitis, asthma, and fevers. In China, calamus is ingested to relieve constipation and swelling. Walt Whitman wrote 45 ballads under the title "Calamus" in his *Leaves of Grass:*

Calamus taste
(For I must change the strain—these are not to
be pensive leaves, but leaves of joy),
Roots and leaves unlike any but themselves,
Scents brought to men and women from the
wild woods, and from the pond-side...

(Calamus No. 13)

Chemistry

The essential oil of calamus contains the psychoactive substances asarone and β-asarone. These are the non-amine precursors to TMA-2, a phenethylamine having 10 times the potency of mescaline.

1, 2, 4-Trimethory-5-propenylbenzene (asarone)

Another possible source of asarone is the wild carrot of Central Asia (*caucus carota*). Asarone is converted to TMA-2 in the body by aminezation which occurs shortly after ingestion.

Primary Effects

Stimulant when a dried root 2" long and the thickness of a pencil is eaten; an **hullucinogen** when over 10" is eaten.

Preparation

Most preferred technique; eat the raw root. The root is much like ginger when dry, both in taste and texture. Your tongue becomes numb after eating it for a period of four minutes. A common tonic recipe is to boil 1 ounce calamus root in 1 point of water. Drink daily before meals. The asarone is more easily converted to TMA-2 on an empty stomach. Root deteriorates with age. They should not be used after they are two years old. The asarone has, by that time, altered itself to be useless.

Ritual Use

One of the constituents of an ointment which Moses was commanded to rub on his body when approaching the Tabernacle:

> Moreover the Lord spoke to Moses, saying 'Take thou also unto thee the chief spieces, of flowing myrrh five hundred shekels, and of sweet cinnamon half so much, even two hundred and fifty, and of sweet calamus two hundred and fifty, and of cassia five hundred, after the shekel of the sanctuary, and of olive oil a kin. And thou shall make it a holy anointing oil, an essence compounded after the art of the perfumer; it shall be a holy anointing oil.'
>
> EXODUS 30:22-25

The psychoactive aspects of asarone in small quantities create the effect of a stimulant. It is for this reason that nearly all Cree Indians over the age of 40 in northern Alberta chew calamus regularly in small amounts as an anti-fatigue medicine. In larger amounts it can be used as a mind-altering sacrament for the Initiation of a boy into a Warrior. It is a stimulant sacrament, used as a tonic for alleviating fatigue.

Note of Caution: *Some experiments indicate that large enough quantities may produce tumors in rats. The amount given to produce this effect is astronomical to the weight of the rat.... No ill effects have been reported in* **any** *of the Cree who use it daily. In fact, they seem to have better health, a statement on health versus healing.*

In England during the 1930's depression, calamus root was chewed as a tobacco substitute. It kills the craving for nicotine because of the ginger taste and aminezation which occurs.

71

Galangal Root

Family: Zingiberaceae (Ginger family).

Botanical Name: *Kaempferia galanga.*

Synonyms: Maraba, catarrh root, China root, India root, colic root.

Geographical Location: Tropical Africa, India, southern China and western Malaysia.

Habitat: Usually in open grassy areas.

Botanical Description: A smooth stemless herb that can grow to the height of about five feet, the leaves are long, narrow blades that spread out horizontally. The flowers form a terminal spike and are white with deep red veining. The rhizome forms branded pieces that look somewhat like ginger that are dark reddish-brown externally that becomes darker towards the center.

History

There are vague reports that maraba is used hallucinogenically by natives in several parts of New Guinea. The rhyzome of *galanga,* rich in essential oils, is highly prized as a condiment and folk medicine in the more tropical regions of Asia. In the Philippines, for example, the rhizome, when mixed with oils, is employed as a poltice and is applied to boils and furuncles to bring them to a head. It has a long history of medicinal use.

Chemistry

Unidentified principles in volatile oils of rhizome. The rhizome has been used in Ginger Beer in England, however, and personal experience indicates interesting alkaloids are present.

Primary Effects

Very mild but real hallucinogen.

Preparation

1) Eat the whole root, approximately 3 inches per person.

2) A tablespoon of the root, cut small, to a cup of boiling water. Drink cold.

Ritual Use

It is recommended that you see the movie *The Valley, obscured by clouds* (music by Pink Floyd). The drug is used in the movie and it is apparent why New Guinea is obscure....

Aleister Crowley uses galangal in his formula for the *incense of Abremelin* in Liber AL III-23. This incense is used in Liber Samekh, a ritual designed for "Knowledge and Conversation" with your Holy Guardian Angel.

Note of Caution: *None available.*

Galangal is a stimulant and aromatic, somewhat similar to ginger, which indicates its uses as a perfume.

      8 parts Cinnamon oil.
      4 parts Myrrh oil.
      2 parts Galangal oil.
      7 parts Olive oil.

A sacrament for welcoming special
guests and friends

Kava Kava

Family: Piperceae (Pepper family).

Botanical Name: *Piper methysticum* Forst.

Synonyms: Kowa, awa, yagona, kowa kowa, wati, ava, ava pepper, intoxicating pepper.

Geographical Location: Polynesia, Sandwich Islands, South Sea Islands.

Habitat: Grows best up to 1000 feet above sea level in cool, moist highlands or wet forests. It will grow densely to 20 feet where summer temperatures are between 80 and 90 °F. with sufficient sunlight.

Botanical Description: An indigenous shrub several feet high with heart-shaped leaves and very short spikes arising from the base of the leaf-stems that are densely covered with flowers. The stem is dictiotomous, that is, two-forked, with spots. The upper rhyzome is the part of the plant that is used and is starchy with a faint pleasant odor with a pungent bitter taste.

Five varieties are cultivated in Fiji, three white and two black. The white varieties are considered best source, but mature one year later than the black. The black are preferred for the commercial crop.

History

Kava kava has a history of religious and spiritual implications in the affairs of men. The following legend summarizes man's relationship to the sun, sky, water, and earth as well as the "Divine Being" or mortal Self and the life cycle. This is the alchemical marriage of fire, wind, water and earth to the spiritual "other" of the soul.

The annual sun sacrifice of a girl of great beauty, Ui, was offered. The Sun was so pleased he took her for his wife. After a period, consent was given for her to return to her people to give birth to their Child. Ui was sent flying through the sky and miscarried. The fetus, however, floated upon the water and was cared for by a hermit crab. The child, Tagaloa Ui, when he grew up, taught mortals how to make Kava as well as Reverence for the ceremony.

Pava, the first mortal participant, had a son who laughed watching his father chew and spit the brew. Tagaloa Ui, angry at the irreverence, cut Pava's son in two. He then gave Pava the correct procedure. Pava then offered the drink to Tagaloa Ui. Instead of drinking it, Tagaloa Ui poured half of the brew on the head son of Pava's, uttering "Soyva" (Life) making the boy whole again. The legend is continued as part of the kava ceremonies of the Samoans even today.

Chemistry

Active component in kava are six resinous alpha pyrones: kawain ($C_{14}H_{14}O_3$) dihydrokawain, methysticin ($C_{15}H_{14}O_5$), dihydromethysticin, yangonin ($C_{15}H_{14}O_3$) and dihydroyangonin. None of these are water soluable

Kawain

except when emulsified. They are soluable in alcohol, oil and other fat sovents, including gastric juices.

Primary Effects

Small amounts produce euphoria; larger amounts produce extreme relaxation, lethargy or lower limbs and eventually sleep. It does not impair mental alertness. Often there are visual and auditory hallucinations, lasting 2-3 hours with no hangover. Kava is similar to marijuana as effects are not noticed when used for the first several times. As a narcotic, Kava later produces numbing of the mouth, similar to cocaine.

Preparation

The part of the Kava plant just below the surface of the ground reaches 3-5 inches thick in 2½-4 years. After 6 years, the root will weigh as much as 20 pounds, after 20 years, 100 pounds. After harvesting, the rootstocks are scraped, cut into pieces, and dried in the sun on platforms.

Traditionally, the root was made into a tea. With the water-soluable components released, it acted as a mild stimulating tonic. If the material is first chewed, then spit into a bowl and mixed with coconut milk, more powerful narcotic-type resins are released in emulsion. For maximum effects, mix 1 ounce Kava with 10 ounces of water (preferably coconut milk), two tablespoons coconut oil or olive oil, and 1 tablespoon lecithin. Blend until the liquid takes on a milky appearance. Serves 1-2 people.

Resins may be extracted with isopropyl (rubbing) alcohol in a heat bath. The solvent is removed by evaporation. Redissolve in just enough warmed brandy, rum, vodka, or honey. This is a more potent method because alcohol swiftly carries the resins into the system.

Ritual Use

Kava's history and chemistry indicate that its euphoria qualities are best shared with special guests or friends. The narcotic affects the "Feeling" centers where warm emotions are generated toward those involved in the ritual. Therefore, Kava has been used as a sacrament for welcoming special guests and friends.

The following ritual is designed for maximum results:

a) Kava or its extracts should be put into your finest glassware (or coconut cups if you have them) and served, to the most revered guests, first. The bearer holds the cup at waist level with thumbs and index finger encircling the outside of the cup.

b) The cup is then lifted to his forehead while in the center of the room. The cup bearer then stops four feet in front of the guests, lets the cup rest in his right palm and lowers his right hand with his left. The left hand is placed behind the back while serving the cup to his guests. He then returns to the center of the room while the guest drinks.

c) The guest receives the cup with both hands, pours a little kava onto the floor and says: "May our Guardians be with us today." He raises the cup and says: "Life" and all others say: "Blessed Be." He then drinks his kava in one gulp. The others are then served. They say nothing, but receive the cup and drink in one gulp.

d) If one accepts kava, but does not finish it, the remainder must be discarded before returning the cup.

e) When all have drunk, the lead guest says: "The ceremony is complete. The bowl will hang with the cup and strainer." Light food should then be served and the party started.

Note of Caution: *Continual chewing eventually destroys tooth enamel. Constant and excessive use of the fresh root with alcohol can become habit-forming and after several* *months results in yellowing of the skin, bloodshot and weak eyes, emaciation, diarrhea, rashes, and scaly, ulcerous skin. When discontinued, the symptoms disappear within two weeks.*

Kawain also has surface anesthetic properties similar to cocaine alkaloids. In the Islands, kava leaves are often applied to cuts and bruises to prevent infection and promote healing. The kava pyrones have antibacterial activity against gonococcus and coli bacilli.

A love sacrament for pagan matrimony
or sexual intercourse

Yohimbe

Family: Rubiaceae (Madder family).

Botanical Name: *Corynanthe yohimbe.*

Synonyms: Pausinystalia yohimba, yohimbehe, johimbe.

Geographical Location: Tropical West Africa, especially the French Congo and the Camerrons.

Habitat: Jungle forests, low altitude.

Botanical Description: A large tree that grows from twelve to sixteen meters in height. The leaves are eight to twelve centimeters in length and are oblong and oval in shape. The seeds are winged.

History

Most of the Bantu-speaking tribes have traditionally used the inner shavings of the bark as a stimulant and aphrodisiac. It is only used when mate-rituals occur. These orgy rituals have been known to last up to 10-15 days, with gradually increased doses.

Chemistry

The active constituents are yohimbine, yohimbiline and ajmaline, all being indole-based alkaloids. The major

Yohimbine

alkaloid yohimbine can also appear as hydrochloride. This makes it easily assimilable via muccous membrances (snorted) or when applied beneath the tongue.

Yohimbine and yohimbiline must react with the hydrochloric acid in your digestive juices for them to become soluble and be assimulated into your body. Yohimbine hydrochloride is also known as quebrachine.

Primary Effects

Yohimbe acts both as a central stimulant and a mild hallucinogen. Yohimbine is a sympatho-mimetic indole-type alkaloid with cholinergic and adrenergic blocking properties. It also inhibits seratonin, the "fine tuning" chemical of the brain.

The first effects are a lethargic weakness of the limbs and a vague restlessness, similar to the initial effects of LSD. Chills and warm spinal shivers may also be felt with slight dizziness and nausea. This is a similar reaction and effect as MDA. Then the effects produce a relaxed and somewhat inebriated mental and physical feeling, accompanied by slight auditory/visual hallucinations. Spinal ganglia is then affected causing erection of the sex organs. The trip lasts from two to four hours.

Preparation

There are several techniques for preparing yohimbe. The traditional way per person is to bring two cups of water to a boil. One ounce of yohimbe is then added to the boiling water and allowed to boil for less than four minutes. The heat is then turned down and the brew simmered for 20 minutes. Strain the liquid and sip slowly about one hour before desired effects.

If you add 1000 mg of ascorbic acid (Vitamin C), the bark tea will react to form yohimbine and yohimbiline ascorbate. This is very soluble forms of the two alkaloids. The alkaloids are more efficient in this state in that they are more quickly assimilated by the body and tend to reduce the possible nausea. It is also recommended that you fast an 18 hour period before ingestion.

The second technique is much more efficient. For one person, soak one ounce of yohimbe bark shavings in ethyl alcohol or any drinking alcohol (gin or vodka works well) for an 8 hour period. Strain the shavings and pour the liquid onto a flat sheet and let the alcohol evaporate. You may use low heat (150-250 °F.) with your oven to speed evaporation. The residue, amounting to 1-1½ grams will be yohimbine hydrochloride. This can be snuffed or placed under the tongue. The effects are more pronounced and the reaction occurs within 10-20 minutes, rather than one hour.

Ritual Use

Yohimbe is the finest sacrament that can be used for a pagan wedding ceremony. A pagan is generally considered as a non-Christian who still uses the concept of a duality. Where Christianity uses the duality of good/evil, the pagan draws their energy from the duality of male/female. One type of pagan altar is arranged by marking a circle on the ground, preferably outside, large enough to surround those who will participate in the ceremony. The altar is set in the center of this circle. An incense burner and six candles are then placed on the altar. One candle is set at each quarter and two remain on the altar during the rite. An image is chosen by the two to be handfasted and this is also placed on the altar with a wand, usually fashioned from a willow branch. The image and the material of the wand are really your choice.

The marriage rite is best performed at the time of the new moon, when energy (soma) is flowing inward rather than outward. For this type of ritual, the altar is usually placed at the eastern edge of the ritual area. All candles are generally white for this ritual and the incense should be of a flower scent, the couple's choice.

The ancient Celtic custom is that the bride wear a veil or net, and an article of red or scarlet. The couple should each obtain and wrap a gift to the other. These are placed on the altar before the ceremony. Wine and cakes should also be present for the orgy to follow. The pledge rings are fitted over the wand and given to the priest/priestess before the ritual.

To begin, the priest or priestess lights the candles and incense. They stand with their backs to the altar (facing west), the priestess to the right of the priest. The priest then holds his right hand aloft and says:

> May the place of this rite
> be consecrated before the Gods.
> For we gather here in a ritual of love
> with two who would be handfasted
> _____ and _____ come forward
> and stand here before us
> and before the gods of nature.

The man and woman step forward, the man to the right of the woman. The priestess says:

> O beings of Air, Be with us here.
> With your clever fingers
> tie closely the bonds between these two.
>
> O beings of Fire, Be with us here.
> Give their love and passion
> your own all-consuming ardor.
>
> O beings of Water, Be with us here.

86

Give them the deepest of love
and richness of body, of soul, and of spirit.

O beings of Earth, Be with us here.
Let your strength and constancy
be theirs for so long as they desire to
remain together.

Bless Goddess and Laughing God
Give to these before us, we do ask,
Your Perfect Love and Perfect Peace.
Blessed Be.

All: Blessed Be.

The priest then picks up the wand and rings and
holds one end of it before him in his right hand, the
priestess does likewise, holding the other end with her left
hand. The rings are between them.

The priestess then says:

Place your right hands
over this wand and your rings.
(His hand over hers).

The priest then says:

Above you are the stars
below you the stones.
As times does pass, Remember...
Like a star should your love be constant.
Like a stone should your love be firm.
Be close, yet not too close.
Possess one another, yet be understanding.
Have patience each with the other
for storms will come, but they will go quickly.
Be free in giving of affection and warmth.
Make love often, and be sensuous to one another.

Have no fear, and let not the ways
of the unenlightened give you discomfort.
For the Goddess and the God are with you
Now and always.

Pause for several seconds, then the priestess says:

Is it your wish _____
to become one with this man?
(Answer)
Is it your wish _____
to become one with this woman?
(Answer)

Does any say nay?

Then as the Goddess, the God, and the
Old Ones are witness to this rite,
I now proclaim you primates!

The yohimbe is now consumed to **seal** the contract
and a kiss is given (The third password).
Now everyone else consumes yohimbe. When the
gifts have been opened, the ritual is considered to be
ended. The priestess then takes the wand and taps each
candle to put it out, starting at the north and going clock-
wise, while saying:

Our rite draws to an end.
O lovely and gracious God and Goddess,
be with each of us as we depart.

The circle is broken!

Then enjoy the evening with your friends and
yohimbe...orgasms will be intensified.
Note: The ritual technique for sexual intercourse is
given with psilocybe mushrooms (page 114).

Note of Caution: *Yohimbe is a MAO inhibitor [monamine
oxidase]. Among the materials which may be dangerous in*

combination with MAO inhibitors are sedatives, tranquilizers, antihistamines, narcotics and large quantities of alcohol...any of these will cause hypotensive crisis [severe blood pressure drop]. Amphetamines, LSD, cocoa, dairy products including aged cheese...any of these will cause hypertensive crisis [severe blood pressure rise]. It is generally recommended that **no other drug** *be used in combination with or within a 10 hour period of the use of yohimbe.*

Librium/or sodium amobarbitol partially block yohimbe effects. Indian snakeroot [*Rauwolfice serpentina*] also contain yohimbine and indole alkaloids. Rauwolfia is not recommended as it takes a minimum of two days to several weeks for the body to metabolize reserpine. There is no control over when the effect will occur. Quite dangerous as an MAO inhibitor.

A sacrament used for initiation
and spiritual growth

Fly Agaric

Family: Agaricaceae (Agaric family).

Botanical Name: *Amanita Muscaria.*

Synonyms: Soma, asumer, amrita (Aryan), pong, pank, pongo (Siberian), bolong gomba (Magyar), Narren Schwamm (German).

Geographical Location: Native to Europe, Asia and North America (north temperate parts of the Eastern and Western Hemispheres).

Habitat: Pine, birch, beech, and larch forests during the rainy seasons (hardwoods, conifer, or fields).

Botanical Description: This marvelous specimen can be found anywhere from one-and-one-half to fourteen inches wide at the cap, forming an ovoid button when young growing nearly flat with age. The cap is red to reddish orange with white warts even when young. Amanita can be found in other colors ranging from orange to light brown to yellow or white, but these species can be considered poisonous. The gills are free and spaced apart and are white in color. A veil is present in young specimens which forms a white collar with age. The spore print is ellipsoid and creamy white. The stem is from one and one-half to twelve inches high by three-eighths to two and one-quarter inches thick and is white to yellowish-white in color with small hairlike tufts along the sides of the stem. The stem is anchored to the ground by a whitish bulb. The inner flesh of the mushroom is firm and white.

History

The name "Fly Agaric" is derived from the Amanita mushroom being used as a decoction to kill flies. Probably the oldest of the halluciogenic plants and perhaps the most widespread, the amanita has been employed for centuries as an orgiastic or shamanistic inebriant by both the Ostyak and Vogul (Finno-Ugrian peoples in western Siberia), the Chukchi, Koryak and Kamchadal of northeastern Siberia, and several Indian tribes along the Pacific Coast. It has even been suggested that the ancient berserker of Scandinavia, who went on periodic orgies of killing, were intoxicated into a mad frenzy by ingesting fly agaric.

An early account of a curious Koryak custom states:

> "When they make a feast, they pour water on some of these mushrooms and boil them. They then drink the liquor, which intoxicates them; the poorer sort, who cannot afford to lay in a store of these mushrooms, post themselves on these occasions round the huts of the rich and watch the opportunity of the guests coming down to make water and then hold a wooden bowl to receive the urine, which they drink off greedily, as having still some virtue of the mushroom in it; and by this way they also get drunk."
>
> Public Health Service Pub. #1645

Some 3,500 years ago, Aryan people came down from the north into the Indus Valley of India, bringing with them the cult of **soma** (the only known plant to be deified). They worshipped this holy inebriant, drinking an extract of it in religious rites. More than 1,000 hymns were composed, in the sacred text known as the **Rig Veda**, 120 of which were devoted exclusively to **soma**. The Aryans were aware of the urine-drinking phenomenon as evidenced by the following quotes:

"Like a stag, come here to drink!
Drink Soma, as much as you like.
Pissing it out day by day, O generous one,
You have assumed your most mighty
force."

VIII 4.10
Rig Veda

"Soma, storm cloud filled with life,
Milked with mild and butter,
Navel of the Path; immortal Concept,
Which springs to life far from here
In unison those charged with the task,
The blessed do honor to Soma.
In flowing movements swollen men piss
Soma."

IX 74.4
Rig Veda

"In the belly of India
Intoxicating Soma is filtered."

IX 80.3
Rig Veda

The Vedic poets speak of three filters involved in the preparation of Soma:

1) The filtering of sunlight into the mushroom, bearing its magical powers from the heavens,

2) The woolen cloth through which the juices were strained,

3) The human body.

John Allegro, in his book *The Sacred Mushroom and the Cross*, working with Sumerian tablets from Arcad and Erech, traces this mushroom through several cultures and finds it to be a focal point in the Christian tradition. One strong point in favor of Allegro's argument is a fresco dating from 1291 on the wall of a deserted church in Plaincourault (Indre, France) which shows Adam and Eve posed on either side of the "Tree of Life" (see cover of book), depicted as a large branched **Amanita** muscaria with a serpent wrapped about it. The forbidden fruit in the mouth of the serpent is clearly an apple. Further data indicates that the entire book of Revelations, written by John the Apostle, was written entirely under the influence of **Soma**, the Fly Agaric!

> "Heaven above does not equal one half of me.
> Have I been drinking Soma?
> In my glory I have passed beyond earth
> and sky.
> Have I been drinking Soma?
>
> I will pick up the earth and put it here or
> there.
> Have I been drinking Soma?

X 119, 7-9
Rig Veda

Chemistry

The main toxic constituents are muscimol, a CNS hallucinogen, ibotenic acid, a precursor to muscimol and muscayone:

Muscarine

Ibotenic acid easily decarboxylates and loses water to be transferred into muscimole at about 165 - 175 °F. Probably muscimole, not a genuine constituent of living **A. muscaria**, is produced mainly during the drying

Ibotenic Acid

$-CO_2$
$-H_2O$

Muscimole

↓ hr

Muscazone

process. UV-irradiation of ibotenic acid results in the production of muscazone.

Other alkaloids present are muscaradine and muscarine. Muscarine, a psychoactive tropane was at one time believed to be responsible for the mental effects of the mushroom. It is now understood to be present in relatively small amounts. It is difficult for this molecule to pass the blood-brain barrier, the third filter of the Vedic poets.

Primary Effects

Dizziness, twitching and possible nausea after 30 minutes followed by numbness of feet and twilight sleep for two hours, hallucinations both visual and auditory. Experience lasts from 4-10 hours. Muscarine is a highly toxic hallucinogen, being a tropane. Muscimole is a CNS hallucinogen. Ibotenic acid causes flushing of the skin and lethargy, or drowsiness.

Preparation

The fresh mushroom should be sliced vertically in ½ inch segments and heated in an oven at 165-175 °F. until dried. The muscarine will mostly evaporate out of the mushroom and the ibotenic acid alters to muscimole. It is recommended that you have a friend available to help you in any emergency. The amount eaten should be conservative, perhaps ¼ to ½ of one mushroom with an 8 inch diameter, until you have personal data on your own body's reaction. *Fasting is critical.* The body does filter the muscarine, so you may wish to save the urine. Mushrooms which dried unplucked in the ground are believed to be the most potent.

Ritual Use

Soma has been regarded as spiritual food, that which aids the growth of the spiritual body. Initiation (where the spirit comes out anew) occurs when this chemistry affects your psychic body. It is a major hallucinogen with nothing to compare. Soma is the "Flesh of the Gods". It is therefore used for Initiation and spiritual growth.

Among the Koryaks the women prepare the mushrooms for the men by moistening and softening them in their mouths and then rolling them in their hands into sausage-shaped morsels. The men either chew these or swallow them whole. Usually three agarics are taken: one large and two small. Sometimes ten to twelve are eaten, but this could easily be a lethal dose.

Mushrooms are also added to soups, sauces, reindeer milk or bogberry (similar to blueberry) juice. The Kamchadals prepare a wine by fermenting a mixture of amanita and this bogberry juice.

The Aryans, as per the Vedic hymns, gathered the mushrooms at night by the light of the full moon. The juices were then pounded out, filtered through a woolen cloth, mixed with water, milk, honey, or a barleycorn infusion, and drunk during magical and religious rites.

The Magickal balance can be seen between muscimole and muscarine: Although they are both hallucinogens, their method on the body is almost precisely opposite. The one counters the affect of the other. One is a food for the spiritual body, the other is a poison for the physical body.

Note of Caution: *Although there are relatively small quantities of muscarine in* **A. muscaria,** *this is not true with other species including* **A. pantherina,** *which is a white-to-yellow-white variety. Identification is extremely important.*

*The standard antidote for muscarine poisoning is atropine. If one of the more lethal amanitas [***A. phalloidso,*** *or* **verna** *or* **A. verosa]** *has been ingested, there may be some chance of saving the victim's life if:*

a) *there is immediate medical attention.*
b) *there is an immediate administration of antitoxin.*
c) *there is a continuous intravenous administration of glucose to maintain the rapidly diminishing bloodsugar level.*

The Koryaks say that if too much agaric has been taken ["leading to pressure on the stomach"*], two to three tablespoons of fat, oil, butter or blubber is an effective remedy. Some tribes believe that a swig of vodka is also helpful.*

The sacrament used for death and rebirth;
the ability to reprogram attitudes,
behavior patterns and goals

Morning Glory Seed

Family: Convovulaceae (Blindweed family).

Botanical Name: *Ipomoea violacea.*

Synonyms: tlitlitzen, badoh negro, badoh, badungas, la'aja shnash, Mexican morning glory, Heavenly Blue, Pearly Gates, Flying Saucers, and Blue stars.

Geographical Locations: Various elevations in North America and Mexico. Other varieties are found in Central and tropical South America. Also in the West Indies.

Habitat: Moist or wet thickets, often weedy in hedges or on the sides of hills and terraces.

Botannical Description: A large vine that often is found clinging to small trees and fences with heart shaped leaves that are membrane-like, four to ten centimeters long by three to eight centimeters wide. The flowers are white and funnel-shaped in dense open clusters. The fruit is a one-seeded capsule oval in shape about thirteen millimeters long.

History

The seeds were said to be used by Aztec priests with ashes of poisonous insects, tobacco, and some live insects as a body rub before sacrifices to make them fearless of their danger. The seed was known as *tlitliltzin*. In their ceremonies a willing victim was thought to be more valuable than an unwilling one, so the sacrament was used to create a more receptive atmosphere to the ceremony. *Tlitliltzin* is the Nahuatl word for black, with a suffix indicating that it was revered as sacred. Hernandez wrote of the morning glory seeds in 1573 and a Spanish record of 1629 reports that the seed in an infusion "deprives a man of his senses and is very powerful". Those who used it were said to have "communicated with the devil, believed in the owl and suck blood".

Today, the Mayatecs grind the seeds in a vietate, wrap the meal in a linen bag and soak it in cold water. The decoction is fairly potent and provides a curandera (healer) with information about the illness possessing their patient. It has also been used to locate lost objects.

Chemistry

Active ingredients are d-lysergic and d-isolysergic acid amides, lysergol, chanoclavine, elymoclavine and ergonovine. D-lysergic acid amide is the principle

Lysergol

Chanoclavine

100

Ergonovine

alkaloid. It is present in the seed in the form of a salt and is, therefore, soluble in water, but not in ether or alcohol, unless it is first hydrolyzed with a 10% amonium hydroxide solution. The alkaloid is also present in the

$R = NH_2$
(Ergine)

d-Lysergic acid amide

$R = NH_2$
(Isoergine)

d-Isolysergic acid amide

Elymoclavine

leaves and stems, but in lesser concentrations than in the seeds. The effects of these alkaloids in combination is similar to LSD and other hallucinogens except their effect is about 10x weaker.

Primary Effects

LSD-like experience lasting from 6-12 hours. There may be some slight nausea, similar to that from peyote. This can be easily eliminated by fasting and taking two or three air sickness pills. Dramamine is recommended.

Preparation

The most successful technique, in consideration to the chemistry involved is:

1) Fast 18 hours before ingestion.

2) When prepared for the ritual, grind the seeds in a pepper grinder. They must be powdered or they will pass through the body with little or no effect.

3) This powder should be placed in a small saucer of water and soaked for one hour. Use ½ ounce per person with a weight of 150 pounds. Three hundred seeds are equal to about 300 micrograms of LSD-25.

4) While you are waiting for the seeds to soak, eat 2-3 dramamine (air sickness pills). A librium or scullcap tea should also be taken at this time to eliminate anxiety.

5) Put the water and the powdered seeds into a milkshake and drink. The first effects will be noticed within 15-45 minutes.

6) When you are beginning to "come down" (Third Bardo) a librium or scullcap tea should again be taken to smooth entry.

Ritual Use

Whenever a person takes a major mind-alterant, they are actually performing an act of Magick. The first, and most important question which should be asked is‘ "Why are you performing this act?" In other terms: "What is the Goal?" Classical Hinduism suggests four possibilities:

1) For increased personal power, intellectual understanding, improvement of life situation or insight into "self".

2) For duty, to help others, providing care or rehabilitation. Healing.

3) For fun, sensuous enjoyment and pure experience.

4) For transcendence, liberation from the three basic illusions: space, time, and ego. Attainment of mystical union.

Once a goal has been selected and defined, the next most important question should then be asked: "What is your method of reprogramming?" I recommend *The Psychedelic Experience* by Timothy Leary. This manual guides one through the intermediate stages between death and rebirth....

It systematically lists the levels of consciousness met after the normal consciousness leaves the place of routine reality. It attempts to forwarn and prepare the voyager for the range of visions to be encountered. Leary's manual is based on the **Bardo Thodol** (often called the *Tibetan Book of the Dead*).

The **Bardo Thodol**, which first appeared in English as the *Tibetan Book of the Dead* in 1927, is used in Tibet as a breviary to be read or recited on the occasion of death to help the dying man concentrate on the experience he is about to undergo. It is like a roadmap to the cycles of events after death which leads *either* to liberation or reincarnation.

In highly symbolic language, the dead man's spirit is told what to expect in each of the three stages between death and rebirth. The first stage describes the psychic happenings at the moment of death; the second stage describes the dream-state which follows and the "karmic" illusions which occur; and the third step describes the beginnings of pre-natal feelings...the return of the ego.

Leary's *The Psychedelic Experience* is the most perfect book written for this form of Magick. He has modularized each point correctly with the ability to *literally* create rebirth! With this manual, one can actually reprogram attitudes, behavior patterns and goals in life. Everyone should experience a controlled programmed LSD trip once in their life...it is a form of Initiation.

Note of Caution: *Persons with any serious history of hepatitis or other liver disorders should not take* **lysergic acid amides.** *Also, egonovine has uterus-stimulating properties. It is given almost routinely to women at the end of the second stage of labor to cause uterine contractions and reduce bleeding. This is why the literature warns in the use of hallucinogens when one is pregnant. You could abort. This does not necessarily apply to pure LSD.*

A list of LSD-like compounds is given for better reference:

Bufotenin — An indoleamine from a plant, *piptadenia peregrina*, and a South American toad. Action similar to LSD.

Caapi (wild rue) — From *Banestericopsis caapi*, a South American jungle vine; contains harmine.

Cohoba (Niopo; parica) — From *Acacia niopo*, a Central American mimosa; contains bufotenin and other substances.

Harmine (banisterine; yageine; telepathine) — From *Peganum harmala* and other plants. Called a psychic sedative. Potent MAO inhibitor.

Iboga — From *Tabermanthe iboga*, an African plant containing ibogaine and ibogamine. Said to relieve fatigue.

Methyltrytamine (indole amphetamine) — Produces rise in serotonin in brain, as does LSD.

Myristicin — From nutmeg, produces bazarre CSN symptoms.

N, N-dimethyltryptamine — Powerful hallucinogen, 5x as active as mescaline; effects appear in 3-5 minutes and disappear in 1 hour. Strong MAO inhibitor.

Psylocybin — will be covered in another part of this book in detail (page 107).

Yage — From *Haemadictyon amayonia*; contains harmine. Stimulates then depresses with drowsy hallucinations.

Hawaiian wood rose seed — large and small — from *Merremia tuberosa* and *nervosa*. I have decided not to discuss this series because I believe morning glory to be a superior species. *M. Nervosa* has a natural coating on the seed which is related to strychnine and must be sanded off...it does not burn off or dissolve in coca cola! Also, the black-brown bark of both seeds must also be removed. The primary alkaloids are identical to that in morning glory seeds. For same results, eat 15 seeds for a bodyweight of 150 pounds.

OLOLVIQUE

BABY WOOD ROSE

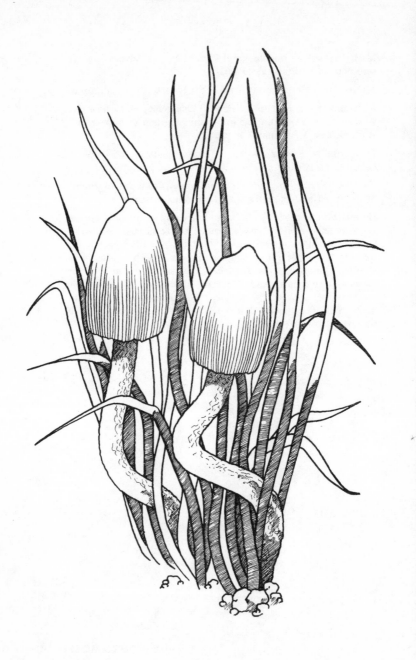

*A sacrament for Sex Magick rituals,
love feats, and prophecy*

Psilocybe Mushroom

Family: Agaricaceae (Agaric family).

Botanical Name:
- a) *Psilocybe Baeocystis.*
- b) *P. Cyanescens.*
- c) *P. Pelliculosa.*
- d) *P. Semilanceata.*
- e) *P. Strictipes.*

Synonyms:
- a) Magick Mushroom.
- b) Strophana.
- c) Elf's Stool.
- d) Liberty Cap.
- e) Cultivator's Cap.

Geographical Location: North and South America, in abundance. There have just recently been reports of identification in New Zealand and China.

Habitat:
- a) Open lawns or near evergreens, especially conifers in the forests.
- b) Found in groups among leaves in woods, lawns and decomposing wood.

c) Grouped in clusters on debris and humus in or near conifer forests.
d) Large groups in tall grass, pastures along the road (never in dung), golf courses.
e) Conifer or mixed woods on the earth or rotting wood.

Botanical Description:

Psilocybe Baeocystis:

Cap: ½" to 2-1/8" wide. Blunt rounded cone-shaped with incurved edge when young, finally expanding to a flat wavy edge with age. Color is olive brown to buff brown with a greenish tinge at the edge, with age. Sticky when wet from a thin separable jelly-like film. Has a slight point in center which is copper brown when dry. The mushroom *Naematoloma* is yellow-capped and should be avoided.

Gills: Almost entire width of gill is attached to stem. Faces are dark cinnamon or gray with purple tints, becoming lavender gray with age. The mushroom *Agaricus* has free gills, although the spore print is similar.

Spore Print: 10 to 13.3 micron by 6.3 to 7 micron. Terete. Purple/lavender gray. *Galerina*, a poisonous mushroom which looks similar, has brown spores. *Omphalina* has white spores.

Stem: 2" to 2 3/4" tall by 1/16" to 1/8" thick. Fibrous, loosely packed, white, becoming cream to yellow at the top. Veil present.

Flesh: Stem is brown. Cap is yellow but lighter than surface. No odor or taste. Stains green.

Season: The end of July through February in some warmer winters.

Note: This species contains larger quantities of psilocybin. This is also the only known species to contain baeocystin and norbaeocystin, representing earlier stages of psilocybin development. Physiological activity has not yet been determined. I see this species as the most potent of the local psilocybins.

Psilocybe Cyanescens:

Gap: 3/4" to 3" wide. Bluntly rounded cone-shaped when young, becoming convex with a knob in the center with age. Color is chestnut when wet.

Gills: Far apart with dark umber faces and pale edges. Faces are cinnamon to dark smoky reddish brown as spores mature.

Spore Print: 9 to 12 micron by 5.5 to 8.3 micron by 5 to 7.7 micron. Distinct and thick-walled. Purple-brown spore, where *psilocybe cubensis* is more purple.

Stem: 2 5/16" to 4" tall by 1/8" to 9/32" stick. Stiff. Base is enlarged and often curved. Covered with silky fibers. Overall color is whitish. Veil is thin and snow white near the cap.

Flesh: White, staining blue when bruised or dried. No odor but tastes similar to fresh grain. One dry gram of this species yields about 2 milligrams of psilocybin. Very potent.

Season: End of July through the end of September.

Note: There are at least two species resembling *psilocybe cyanescens* that have not yet been formally identified and named.

Psilocybe Pelliculosa

Cap: 5/16" to 1 3/16" wide, at least half as high as wide. Bluntly rounded cone-shaped with straight edge when young. Becomes bell-shaped with age. Color is yellow-brown to olive when young. Fades to dull pale brownish yellow with greenish gray tint with age. Sticky when wet from separable jelly-like film (appears translucent with radial lines from edge when wet).

Gills: Close and connected to stem. Separates with age. Edged almost white, faces are dull cinnamon brown until darkened by spores.

Spore Print: 9.3 to 13 micron by 5 to 7 micron. Distinct pore, smooth, terete to ellipsoid. Purple-brown spore.

Stem: 2 5/16" to 3 1/8" tall by 1/16" thick at the top. Color is white to grayish. Covered with silky fibers, brownish toward the lower portion. Dark brown with age. Upper portion covered with powdery secretion. Veil generally absent. Stem larger at base.

Flesh: Thin and pliant at the cap. Tough stem. Both become bluish green when bruised. Odor is slightly musty.

Season: End of August through January.

Note: Although this species is small, do not let that influence your desire to hunt it. *Psilocybe mexicana*, the most highly prized of the Mexican species is even smaller!

Psilocybe Strictipes:

Cap: 3/4" to 1 5/8" wide. Bell shaped to convex when young. Becomes broadly convex to flat with wavy edge with age. Color is dull yellowish brown to olive brown. Fades to cinnamon buff in center and almost white at the edge. Then dingy overall with age. Film of jelly-like material present when wet. Stains green.

Gills: Close, with three tiers of partial gills, connected to stem. Faces are white but become dark chocolate brown from spores.

Spore Print: 9 to 12 micron by 5.5 to 6.5 micron. Smooth with pore. Purplish brown spore.

Stem: 3 1/2" to 5 1/8" tall by 5/64" to 1/8" thick. Straight, stuffed with pale brownish pith. Surface almost white from closely pressed fibers. Stains brownish where fibers are removed.

Flesh: Cap same color as surface, dingy brownish and brittle in outer layer of stem. No odor. Tastes mild. Stains bluish green.

Season: The end of September through November only.

Note: This species is very similar to *psilocybe baeocystis* but has a longer stem.

For a complete description of all the hallucinogenic mushrooms, see *Magickal Mushroom Handbook* by Richard Miller. (Available from Beltane Herb Company, 2311 N. 45th., Seattle, Washington 98103).

History

R. Gordon Wasson has presented evidence depicting mushroom worship dating to AD 300. Mushroom stone images have been found from Guatemala dating back to perhaps 1000 B.C. Some of these stones depict a young woman sitting under a mushroom with a metate. Although they were formerly thought to be connected with a form of phallic workship (due to their peculiar form), they are now associated with the ancient mushroom rites.

Mushrooms were doubtlessly consumed in rituals over much of Central America in ancient times, but the only tribe which is definitely known to have used teonanacatl ("Flesh of the Gods") is the Chichimecas. There are six tribes in Oaxaca today who consume sacred mushrooms: Mazatecs, Chinantecs, Chatinos, Zapotecs, Mixtecs, and Mijes. Other tribes using sacred mushrooms are the Nahoas of Mexico, the Tarascans of Michoacan, and the Otomis of Puebla.

Chemistry

All psilocybe mushrooms contain the hallucinogen alkaloids psilocybin and psilocin.

Psilocybin

Psilocin

As noted in the special note on *P. Baeocystis*, this species has also been found to contain baeocystin and norbaeocystin. These alkaloids are believed to interfere with the respiratory system, so it is recommended that they be used with caution.

Baeocystin

Norbaeocystin

Primary Effects

Colored hallucinations, muscular relaxation, hilarity, inability to concentrate one's attention, alteration of time and space perception and feelings of total isolation from the environment. Peak occurs 1-1½ hours after ingestion. Total experience is approximately 6 hours.

Preparation

There is really no preparation other than making sure all manure or dirt is off the mushroom. They should **not** be stored in a plastic baggie and frozen. If you wish to store them, the only correct way is to string them by their stem and hang them upside down, free to air dry.

Once they have completely dried, then they can be powdered and placed in a bag which can "breath". The best way to serve the dried mushroom is to powder it and mix it with a favorite liqueur. Heat over 150 °F. will destroy much of the psilocin. In other words, spaghetti dinners are nice only if the mushrooms are added to the sauce *at the last moment.*

Ritual Use

Sex Magick: The first use of sex within the rituals of western traditions of Magick began with the Ordo Templi Orientis (O.T.O.), an 800-year-old Masonic order in Germany. They had studied the Hindu traditions of tantra and found that the energy contained in those rituals were greater than any known technique. At the turn of the century, Aleister Crowley became their new Outer Head of the Order (O.H.O.) and rewrote those rituals for a more contemporary application. For a clear picture of this technique, it is recommended that the sutdent first read chapter 16 of *The Tree of Life* by Israel Regardie. Then read pages 82-86 of *Liber Aleph, The Book of Wisdom or Folly* by Aleister Crowley. From page 86:

"de Formula Tota
on the complete formula

Here then is thy Schedule for all Operations of Magick. First: thou shalt discover thy True Will, as I have already taught thee, and that Bud therefore which is the Purpose of this Operation.

"Next, formulate this Bud-Will as a Person, seeking or constructing it, and naming it, according to thine Holy Qabalah, and its infallible Rule of Truth.

"Third: Purify and consecrate this Person, concentrating upon him, and against all else. This Preparation shall continue in all thy daily Life. Mark well: make ready a New Child immediately after every Birth.

"Fourth: make an especial and direct Invocation at thy Mass, before the Introit, formulating a visible Image of this Child, and offering the Right of Incarnation.

"Fifth: perform the Mass, not omitting the Ipiklesis, and let there be a Golden Wedding Ring at the Marriage of thy Lion with thine Eagle.

"Sixth: at the Consumption of the Eucharist accept this Child, loosing thy Consciousness in him, until he be well assimilated within thee.

"Now then do this continuously, for by Repetition cometh forth both Strength and Skill, and the Effect is cumulative, if thou allow no time for it to dissipate itself."

What Crowley has described is known as the "Mass of the Holy Ghost". I will now describe in simple terms how this formula is applied to sex magick:

Discover your True Will. What is the Purpose of the Operation? Do you need money? Or perhaps you wish to have some event occur, etc.

"Name it" ...as a person, an entity which has its own personality. It could be that wish to change a habit within yourself. If that is the case, then treat this new proposed change as a **new** entity, a **new** person which is not you. This is the detail to the purpose.

Purify and consecrate this new person. This is the point where you and your mate generate the Desire...the foreplay with each reminding the other continuously of the Purpose of the Operation. This is the Bud-Will.

Formulate an image of this Bud-Will into a child (a Magickal Child). With entry, you both begin to redefine the Child. This is properly called *synergy:* the creation of new information to add and supplement the original Intent. It is the Invocation. You begin to live what you create. For visualization, the Red Lion is the male essence and the White Eagle is the female menstruum.

Form the bond with a gold ring. This is the climax! The Red Lion becomes the White Lion and the White Eagle becomes the Red Eagle.

Note: *The thought during a sexual climax...happens!* (This is the Masonic secret)

Consume the eucharist, eat it and know that no other energy is necessary. After the climax, both male and female should eat the semen and menstruum. The eucharist in alchemical terms is the Philosopher's Stone!

Repetition of the thought and act brings Strength and Skill.

In this ritual it should be noted that only **odd** numbers of mushrooms should be eaten for this ritual, never even numbers.

Mexican Love Feast: Each adult takes either 4, 5, 6, or 13 pairs of mushrooms and experiences his or her own inner ecstacy while sharing feelings of brotherly love with the others. The curandero may chant or dance periodically during this event.

Mexican Prophecy Ritual: Before the ceremony a chocolate beverage like cocoa is usually served. Women sing, dance and clap hands. The curandero gathers some corn, parrot feathers, cacao beans, copal resin, green tobacco and bark paper. He has fasted since noon of the preceeding day. For five days he has abstained from sex, alcohol, meat and salt. This will continue for another five days after the ritual (Otherwise he believes that he risks going mad). At sunset the altar candles are lit. Those present are seated on the floor. The question for prophesy is decided and clarified. The mushrooms are then eaten in pairs during a period of one hour. As many as 14 pairs can be eaten. No one is allowed to leave. Silence is maintained. The curandero rubs green tobacco on his head and stomach and on the back of his neck. He blows out the candles. At one a.m. in the morning the prophecy begins.

Note of Caution: *Make absolutely positive identification of the species of mushroom to be used. It is a drag eating a poisonous mushroom during Sex Magick rituals. Also note the* **P. Baeocystis** *does have other alkaloids which should not be used by any person who has respiratory problems. In Mexico it is said that the mushroom is capable of driving a person mad if certain precautions are not taken. For this reason pregnant women do not consume the mushroom in Oaxaca.*

Other intoxicating mushrooms are the *Amanita, Conocybe, Panaeolus, Stropharia, Pholiotina* and the Copelandia. All are described in *Magickal Mushroom Handbook* by Richard Miller.

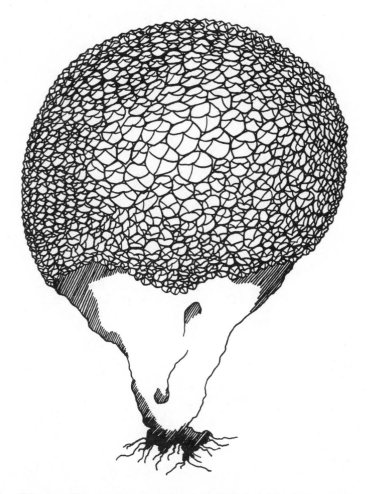

Gi'i-sa-wa [*Lycoperdon marginatum*] Puffball found in the temperate forests of Mexico. Non-visual hallucinogen. Some related species grow wild in the United States.

*A sacrament used
for astral projection*

Thorn Apple

Family: Solanaceae (Nightshade or Potato family).

Botanical Name: *Datura stramonium.*

Synonyms: Jimson weed, devil's apple, stinkweed, Jamestown weed, yerba del diablo, angel's trumpet, Gabriel's trumpet.

Geographical Location: Native to Southwestern U.S., Mexico, Central America, India and Asia.

Habitat: Sandy soil areas, flatlands, open semi-dry low land meadows and roadsides.

Botanical Description: A coarse herb that is annual and branches freely attaining the height of about three feet. It has a long thick and whitish root with many fibers. The stem is smooth and erect with many branches. The leaves which are large and angular four to six inches with a coarsely-toothed margin, grow singly along with one flower in the forks of the branching stems. The flowers are large, about three inches in length, and are encased in a calyx; is long and tubular and swollen below ending in five very sharp teeth. The top part of the flower, called the corolla, is pure white and half-opened in a funnel-shape with six prominent ribs extending into six sharp pointed segments at the top of the flower.

History

The name *datura* originated from early Arabian names such as *datora* and *tatorah*. Early sanskrit writings refer to these drugs as *dhurstura* and *unmata*. The name "Jimson weed" comes from Jamestown, Virginia, where a colonist found *datura* growing near a pile of rubbish from the ships at dock.

In India, women known as "Mundane ladies" (whores) would use "knockout drops" [*D. Metal*] for intoxicating and robbing their clients. It is a powerful narcotic.

Old Chinese herbal medicine texts state that if equal amounts of Jimson weed and *Cannibis sativa* are gathered in the seventh and eighth moon, dried in the shade, pulverized and digested in wine, the preparation

BELLADONNA

ingested would produce a narcotic anesthesia making operations and cauterizations to be accomplished with little or no pain.

Algonkian Indians of eastern North America would make a drink "wysoccan", containing Jimson weed, for young boys to be initiated into manhood. A type of violent madness would occur for about 20 days with a total loss of memory of their former life. When the boy regained consciousness, he would start adulthood forgetting that he was ever a child.

Chemistry

Principle active component is scopolomine (hyoscine). Other alkaloids are atropine, hyosyamine,

Scopolamine Hydrobromide (Hyoscine)

Atropine Sulfate (Tincture of Belladonna)

mandragorine and other tropanes. These are all parasympathetic depressants.

Primary Effects

Parasympathetic depressant. Hallucinogen and hypnotic. A hypnotic produces low alphoid and spindal alpha brain activity. This does not allow deep sleep to occur although it does lower brain patterns to states where dreams occur.

Preparation

DO NOT INGEST!! The leaves are smoked (Don Juan's "little smoke"). *Cannabis sativa* may be added. Dose should be less than 2 grams per session, done less than once per week.

HENBANE

Ritual Use

In 1658, Porta states that a potion containing henbane, mandrake, stromonium and belladonna was drunk to make a man act like a beast—probably one of the origins of lycanthropy.

Traditional techniques for witch's flying ointment was to take the fat of some animal or even a child, simmer it in the fresh juice of stiamonium, water parsnip, aconite, cinquefoil and deadly nightshade. Soot was added to blacken the mixture and then the ointment was rubbed over the entire body. A broom was then sometimes used to put more of the ointment up into the vaginal cavity...by this time the witch was really hallucinating and experienced "flying on her broomstick to the sabbath." This is a classic example of astral projection.

To control the experience of astral projection, the recommended procedure is to fast the day before the experiemnt (drugs also). In the afternoon secure your room from sound and other possible distractions: telephone, visitors, etc. Smoke two large joints of datura, about 1 gram each. Then lay back and allow the "effects" to occur. To get a better example of expected "effects" and what you might do with this experience, I recommend the book *Journies Out of the Body* by Robert Monroe.

Note of Caution: *Datura can be detrimental to the heart because of the tropanes. A tolerance is built up to the tropanes in the parasympathetic system, thus requiring more datura to achieve the same "effects". This is* **not** *true with their effects on the heart and severe damage may occur. This is why this and related tropanes should never be ingested. It is extremely toxic.*

Other tropane containing herbs which may be used similarly are:

    a) Belladonna [*Atropa belladonna*] — also known as deadly nightshade. Used originally to dialate pupils attractively, hence belladonna.

b) Henbane [*Hysocyamus niger*] — also known as devils's eye. Traditional use was as a flying ointment for ritual.
c) Mandrake [*Mandragora officinarum*] — Also known as may apple. Believed to be magical because of its root structure resemblanced that of a man.
d) Monkshood [*Aconitum napellus*] — Also known as wolf's bane or aconite, was traditionally considered to be the most important of the solanaceae group as it was used to fight the vampire.

All of the above can be made into extracts with ethyl alcohol. A smoke is then prepared by dipping a cigarette or herbal into the extract and letting it air dry.

e) Mint Bidis (non tobacco cigarettes from India) — The ingredients are spearmint, gigantic swallow wort, thorn apple, holy basil, marjoram, sour orange, and pappaval (sic). Mint Bidis contains 65 mg scopolamine and 16 mg atropine per cigarette.

MANDRAKE

126

Quick Reference Chart

Common Name	Principle Agent	Suggested Use	Effect
Belladonna	Atropine, scopolomine	Ointment	Strong hallucinogen
Betel Nut	Arecoline	Chew as plug	Stimulant
Broom, Scotch Broom	Cytisine	Smoke	Strong Sedative
Bufotenin	Bufotenin	Ointment	Hallucinogen
Caapi	Harmine	Tea	Stimulant
Calamus	Asarone	Eat	Mild hallucinogen
California Poppy	Glusides	Smoke	Mild euphoriant
Catnip	Nepetalactone	Tea	Mild hallucinogen
Cinnamon	Unknown	Smoke	Mild stimulant
Cohoba	Bufotenin	Ointment	Hallucinogen
Coffee	Caffeine	Tea	Stimulant

Common Name	Principle Agent	Suggested Use	Effect
Conocybe Mushroom	Psilocybin, Psilocin	Eat	Mild hallucinogen
Copelandia Mushroom	Psilocybin, Psilocin	Eat	Mild hallucinogen
Damiana	Unknown	Smoke	Mild stimulant
Ephedra	Ephedrine	Tea	Stimulant
Fly Agaric	Muscimole, muscarine	Eat	Strong hallucinogen
Galangal Root	Rhizome	Tea	Mild hallucinogen
Guarana	Caffeine	Tea	Strong stimulnat
Harmine	Harmine	Tea	Stimulant
Hawaiian Wood Rose	Lysergic Acid Amides	Eat	Strong hallucinogen
Henbane	Atropine, scopolomine	Ointment	Hallucinogen
Hops	Lupuline	Tea	None
Hydrangea	Hydrangin, cyanogenes, saponin	Smoke	Stimulant

Common Name	Principle Agent	Suggested Use	Effect
Iboga	Ibogaine, Ibogamine	Tea	Stimulant
Juniper	Unknown	Smoke	Hallucinogen
Kava, Kava	Kawain, pyrones	Tea	Mild hallucinogen
Kola Nut	Caffeine	Tea	Stimulant
Lobelia	Lobeline	Tea	Mild Euphoriant
Mandrake	Scopolamine	Tea	Hallucinogen
Mate	Caffeine	Tea	Stimulant
Mint Bidis	Atropine, scopolomine	Smoke	Mild hallucinogen
Monkshood	Atropine, scopolamine	Ointment	Hallucinogen
Mormon Tea	Ephedrine	Tea	Stimulant
Morning Glory Seed	Lysergic acid amides	Eat	Strong hallucinogen
Nutmeg	Myristicin	Tea	Mild hallucinogen

Common Name	Principle Agent	Suggested Use	Effect
Panaeolus Mushroom	Psilocybin, Psilocin	Eat	Mild hallucinogen
Passion Flower	Harmine alkaloids	Smoke or tea	Mild stimulant
Periwinkle	Indole alkaloids	Tea	Hallucinogen
Pholiotina Mushroom	Psilocybin, Psilocin	Eat	Strong hallucinogen
Prickly Poppy	Isoquinilines, photopine, bergine	Smoke	Narcotic-analgesic
Psilocybe Mushroom	Psilocybin, psilocin	Eat	Strong hallucinogen
Scullcap	Unknown	Tea	Tranquilizer
Snakeroot	Reserpine	Tea	Tranquilizer
Stropharia Mushroom	Psilocybin, Psilocin	Eat	Hallucinogen
Tea	Caffeine	Tea	Stimulant
Thorn Apple	Atropine, scopolamine	Smoke or tea	Strong hallucinogen
Tobacco	Nicotine	Smoke	Strong stimulant

Common Name	Principle Agent	Suggested Use	Effect
Valerian Root	Chatinine, valerine	Tea	Tranquilizer
Wild Lettuce	Lactucarine	Smoke	Mild narcotic-analgesic
Wormwood	Absinthine	Liqueur	Narcotic-analgesic
Yage'	Harmine	Tea	Stimulant-hallucinogen
Yohimbe	Yohimbine	Tea	Mild hallucinogen

Most all of the botanicals described in this book are legal today.

Herbs and Healers

Primitive healers who practice the traditional medicine of their region are found throughout the world, in such diverse areas as Siberia, Indonesia, Africa, and North and South America. These healers are most frequently referred to as witch doctors, magicians, or shamans. Their natural medical knowledge enables them to use herbs for their curative powers, to treat various injuries, and to enter the spirit world through trance in order to heal the soul of the patient.

In his classic work on shamanism, the Jungian psychologist Mircéa Eliade wrote that these healers defend life, health, fertility, and the world of light against death, sterility, diseases, disaster, and the world of darkness in general. Therefore, the shaman or medicine man is called on in times of spiritual as well as physical adversity.

Just how does one become a shaman with the magical power to heal others? Generally, one first hears a "voice" or gets the calling in the true sense of a vocation. Characteristically this calling comes through a psychological crisis or severe illness, where the threat of death is imminent. The future shaman gets a vision or glimpse of the spirit world, which today we term the deep unconscious. He learns how to draw on the healing power of the psyche to effect his own cure. Part of his training becomes developing the ability to enter or leave this trance state at will.

Once sufficiently recovered from his physical symptoms, the healer begins formal training, which starts with an initiation ceremony. This ceremony differs according to which type of practice the healer will take up. In African societies, for example, there are three types of traditional healers; each is classified by the manner in which plants are used for their medicinal value.

1. *The herbalist* uses the chemical properties of plants to effect a medical cure. He may be an unassuming or colorful individual and enjoys a position of prestige in his community, like a doctor.
2. *The divine healer* attempts to use the spiritual powers of plants to treat his patients. He also relies on entering the trance to evoke his supernatural powers of diagnosis. He is a spiritual healer, or priest.
3. *The witch doctor* uses his powers of exorcism to combat evil. He uses plants thought to have exorcising powers during his treatments. By ridding the patient of his "demons," he functions much like our modernday psychologists and psychiatrists, whom we sometimes refer to as "shrinks," short for "head-shrinkers."

In Ghana, those who fall into the trance and hear the voice may enter into a three-year apprenticeship program to become traditional healers, or herbalists. The new student is taken to a cemetary where it will be easier to contact the spirits of his ancestors. Here he receives a ceremonial bath with water in which several plant species have been soaking. These include African cucumber (*Momordica charantia*), a vine whose yellow fruits are used to treat diabetes and whose leaves are used to treat hypertension. In the West Indies, African cucumber is used to treat rheumatism and fever and for birth control.

After the bath, the initiate is instructed in the taboos, which he must observe. He must remain celibate, abstain from alcoholic beverages, neither quarrel nor fight with anyone, nor go out at night. He is admonished not to evoke the aid of any god to harm another human, and he may not serve the chief of his village or his court, for reasons similar to our separation of church and state. The initiate must dress very simply, perhaps only in a piece of white cloth. He also learns to salute his elders by *bending the right knee and touching the ground with his right hand.*

After the preliminary requirements are fulfilled, training proceeds as follows:

Year 1: The initiate learns how to live a disciplined life, does not mix too freely with the village folk, and neither cuts nor combs his hair.

Year 2: Focus is on herbal training in the forest. The initiate learns the names, descriptions, and uses of plants directly from his instructor. He is shown how to combine different plant parts. For example, the flowers and bark of the African tulip tree (*Spathodea campanulata*) crushed together are used to treat ulcers; a decoction of the leaves is used for gonorrhea; the bark alone is a treatment for kidney problems.

The initiate also receives spiritual instructions from his deity or inner guiding voice. He learns to observe subtleties in the forest and becomes aware of its secrets. For example, he sees how wounded animals go to certain plants for relief.

In the last part of his second year, he learns how to sacrifice to the gods. He adopts ritual adornment around his wrists, ankles, and neck. His hair is decorated with charms.

Year 3: The initiate learns the art of gazing at water in a bowl with intense concentration. As in crystal-gazing, he will perceive the faces of spirits or ancestors and will "hear" their voices, which counsel him concerning his patients. When he can do this proficiently, he makes a secret covenant with his instructor. This consists of taking an oath of allegiance, or mutual fidelity, by licking blood from an incision in his teacher's right wrist; the teacher does the same and so graduates his student as a practitioner.

Other herbs used in traditional medicine around the world include the following: Madagascar periwinkle is used to treat leukemia. The African vine *Strophanthus* yields both poison and a heart stimulant. The Eurasian *Acorus calamus* has both insecticidal and sedative properties. Vines and roots of *Arisolochia ringens* are used in India for digestion and blood pressure. *Annona reticulata*, or custard apple, has remedies for different ailments in its roots, bark, and seeds. *Discorea composita*, a true yam, yields diosgenin for birth control, asthma, and arthritis. *Passiflora coccinea* is used for insomnia in the West Indies because it contains the sedative passiflorine. There are more examples, too numerous to mention.

Just how are these examples of shamanism relevant to our modern life? They are important to know about because we all have a bit of the shaman in us, waiting to be called to the fore to initiate us into the intriguing world of the spirits — or, in modern parlance, the direct experience of the unconscious. When we seek to change our consciousness through the use of herbs or the magic of self-transformation, we seek admittance into the province of the shaman.

The shaman presides over knowledge of the *creative cure*, which seeks out the meaning of an illness for the individual. Whether our ills are physical, psychological, or spiritual, we can call upon our inner resources (the shaman within) for healing and illumination. By calling upon our own creativity, we may succeed in effecting a cure where modern medicine has failed. Fully 85% of all illnesses have been shown to be self-limiting. In many instances, the mystery of healing lies within us.

As stated before, shamans do not confine their

treatment to the use of medicinal herbs. They also attribute a healing power to dreams, providing one pays the proper attention to them. One needn't become ill to obtain initiation, even though illness is one form of initiation. A psychological illness or crisis may, however, call up our deep inner resources, making us more conscious or developed than we were before. It can produce marked changes in personality and give us compassion for the suffering of others. Having had his own personal encounter with the depths of the unconscious, the shaman can help others relate to their personal, inner experiences.

Just how can we tap this source of healing? We may not all become healers, but chances are we will all suffer an illness or be incapacitated at some time. When this happens we must seek the meaning of the illness in our inner self, as well as suffer its infirmities. We can contact our own inner creativity through the process of visualization, or seeing with the mind's eye. The psychological technique of *active imagination* allows for direct experience of the unconscious, but we needn't enter a deep trance to achieve it.

Active imagination goes beyond the visualization of an image — it is an active interaction with it. Water is a symbol of the fluid imagination. Like the shaman's water-gazing technique, we can use active imagination to contact an image, voice, or figure that personifies our unconscious. For example, if we are ill and the doctors are at a loss and cannot help us, we might call up the figure of our inner shaman for advice. Once we can see his form, we will be able to hold a kind of dialogue with it, just like we might in a normal consultation. The inner shaman may advise us on the spiritual meaning of our infirmity, or counsel us to heed our dreams, or suggest we make some talisman or other propitiatory gesture. If it does not conflict with your ethics, be sure to apply any advice obtained in this manner, even if it seems foolish to your "sophisticated" Western mind.

Contact this wisdom figure by sitting quietly in a dimly lit room. Breathe deeply and rhythmically, allowing yourself to relax into a state between sleeping and being awake. This is the brain state where twilight imagery appears most easily, but it is not the trance state where the ego is normally unconscious. It can be thought of as an *imagery* state, rather than a trance state. Progressively deepen your awareness while contemplating the figure of inner wisdom and healing. This figure is in contact with the ultimate meaning of life, and through dialogue with him or her, you may seek a new relationship to the truths of human existence. Formulate a clear picture in your mind of the face of your healer. It may appear as someone you know or have heard of, or as a legendary or cosmic figure, such as Christ, Mary, or Buddha. This figure is a personification of compassion, wisdom, and the power to make you whole.

Close your eyes and feel the presence of the healer. Turn off your conscious thoughts and bask in the warm aura of the wisdom figure. Try to grasp the sensation of extended consciousness that comes with this inner person. When you have the image clearly in mind, greet the inner being and begin speaking about your concerns and questions regarding your illness (whether physical, psychosomatic, or purely psychological). Tell the inner shaman why you have called upon him or her and what you must ask.

Allow the inner figure to speak; listen and record what is said on paper. The shaman may also have probing questions for you to answer. It is important to write down your active imagination, in much the same way that you can record your dreams. This prevents memory from altering the information and makes it seem less elusive or ephemeral. Write down both sides of the dialogue. You may wish to do a bit of active imagination and then write it down. Or, as some prefer, you may wish to keep writing continually, as fast as possible, while the dialogue simply comes to mind. This fast writing, with little regard for grammar, keeps the ego from intruding on the process. Let the dialogue move at its own pace, covering whatever subject matter comes up. Many factors of life may relate to your "dis-ease."

Talk as long as the inner shaman wishes. Mere contact with this figure exerts a certain healing effect on the personality. The healing power radiates from the shaman in a positive analogy to the negative contagious effect of a disease. The inner shaman is a personification of the archetype of meaning. By giving this inner potential an imagined body to inhabit, you will gain the ability to begin a *conscious* relationship with it. By giving it a voice, you allow it to speak with you. If you feel you can only hear the voice but can't see the form, request the shaman to appear before you.

The value of developing this relationship with the figure of inner wisdom and healing is that what was formerly unconscious and pure potential becomes conscious and begins to actualize. The split between the conscious and unconscious aspects of ourselves is the source of much of our discomforts and illness, both physical and psychological. Illness seems to be a psychobiological phenomenon. Any step we can make toward self-knowledge or understanding of our unconscious self works toward healing this split. There is a deeper meaning at work in our lives than the ego is usually aware of. The inner shaman can bring awareness of this deep meaning into consciousness.

This medicine man, witch doctor, magician, priest, or psychic healer may take different forms in your imagination at different times. Perhaps each is suited to a particular ailment. Sometimes your healer may be a woman and sometimes a man. Most often, the healer is seen as the same sex as oneself. Sometimes one is "led" to the figure of the healer by an inner companion of the opposite sex!

The inner guiding spirit of a practicing shaman is feminine and is regarded as his celestial wife. He may

138

also have an earthly wife, providing he gives both the proper attention. This reminds us that the unconscious of a man is partly feminine, and is therefore personified as a woman. The situation is reversed for a shamaness, or female healer. Her familiar spirit will most likely be male, and is considered to be her heavenly husband.

Thus, the shaman gains his healing ability from personal contact with the spirit world, or unconscious, and acquires spiritual potency. His professional training in herbology, primitive surgery, etc., augments his healing powers. But the divine contact is the main source of his power. Anyone can contact this source within himself directly through exercise of the active imagination and dialogue with the inner figure of the healer.

The primary criterion of the shaman is the ability to enter the ecstatic trance. This altered state of consciousness allows him to gain advice from the spirits to heal his patient's soul. A shaman has the capacity to go out of himself at will. This means that he can slough off the conscious personality, take on the role of the shaman, and enter the landscape of inner reality where the relationship between all events and things is revealed. By touching the deep level of inner harmony and returning to the mundane level, he brings some of this sense of wholeness back to the mundane world.

By calling on our inner shaman or healer, we seek to gain contact with our own principle of wholeness and healing. During our attempts at dialogue, there may be long pauses in the conversation. We should not give up, but should sit in stillness, waiting with a feeling of openness and expectation. The dialogue will recharge itself with new energy on an even deeper level. There may be three or four long pauses during the deepening process.

When you feel you've completed a dialogue exercise, read over what you have written of your conversation with the inner shaman. How do you feel as a result of this exercise? Write down your feelings, both physical and emotional. Compare how you feel after reviewing the script with how you felt during its writing. Were you able to suspend the skeptical viewpoint of the ego? The dialogue exercise is now at a close, but your relationship to this figure has just begun. You can repeat the exercise whenever you see fit. Perhaps you found the contact to be stimulating or inspiring. If you feel inspired by the momentum created by the inner wisdom dialogue, you may want to express it in some creative form such as painting, music, dance, writing, or sculpting. Such art projects are an excellent form of active imagination since they are largely nonverbal and influence our being on a symbolic level.

Symbols have the power to influence our deepest subconscious mind. In addition, the symbols spontaneously produced by our own inner transformation process have the ability to heal us. If you experience an image of a profound nature through, for instance, dream or active imagination, hang on to it. Contemplate this symbol for an extended period of time until you can extract its core meaning or individual message for you. When you understand one symbol of transformation, its healing energy will flow into another symbol. In this way, you will become consciously more integrated as you learn the lessons of the unconscious.

In magic, the realm of dream and living symbolism is called the Astral Plane. It is in this realm that shamans have journeys or soul travel. Today we term these Out-Of-Body-Experiences (OOBE) or astral projections. Since symbols are living entities on the astral level, the creation of an impression or form through visualization on this level means that you are initiating its later manifestation on the physical level. Healers can visualize the patient as whole or healed and speed up the healing process.

A shaman must never use his creative ability to instigate illness in another or in any way use his psychic power for personal interest. To do so is considered the lowest form of magic and would jeopardize the shaman's continued ability to function as a healer within his community. A broader description of his duty is to defend the community against evil. To retain his own health, he must serve his spiritual calling, not his ego.

Psychologically, the trance state is considered an archaic mode of primitive consciousness that involves the body in somatic and kinesthetic behavior. There are states of consciousness that exceed the trance state of the shaman in terms of mystical and magical development. Even in our modern society, we all retain this primitive being within ourselves, and this is why it is still possible to call upon the inner shaman for healing. The trance state includes such phenomenal experiences as possession, mediumship, the hypnotic state, astral projection, psychedelic drug episodes, and paranormal aspects such as ESP. Its range extends from the extreme dissociation of schizophrenia to the ecstasy of mystics and the magical flight of shamans. Ego control is weak or absent, and there is a general amnesia concerning the experiences. Trance is the temporary restructuring of reality orientation. It includes the following states:

1. *Sleep.* In this state images are profuse but the ego/will is absent.
2. *Possession.* This is a state where the individual ego is usurped by a malevolent demon or spirit.
3. *Mediumistic trance.* This trance state is a form of possession where a benign (or dead) spirit controls and dominates the individual ego.
4. *Group trance dances* such as those practiced by American Indians, Sufis, and Voodoos. These are also forms of possession, with paranormal manifestations.
5. *Psychedelic drug states.* These experiences provide premature access to the deep unconscious, and even though they provide vivid imaginal "trips," the ego has difficulty recalling them or integrating them meaningfully and cannot repeat them at will.
6. *Sensory deprivation states.* These produce hallucinations and disorientation.

7. *Hypnosis* and *Autohypnosis states.* These produce four classic depths of trance.
8. *Shamanistic trance.* This is a high form of trance. The sorcerer's mission is to influence the environment by magic. He is not possessed by spirits, but controls them. He retains his memory of magical flights or OOBE. He receives and remembers instructions from dreams, and because of his own wounding and recovery has the ability to heal.
9. *Magical trance.* This is a form of "lunar" magic. It uses psychic powers for personal interests. Its form of induction is ritual, and its mode of working is visualization.

Paranormal aspects of the trance state include telepathy, clairvoyance, precognition, psychometry, anesthesia of pain, healing, fire-walking and other mastery over fire, psychokinesis and poltergeist phenomena, astral projection, automatic writing, and psychic surgery. These can all be considered as part of the physical world of phenomena and illusion. *Imagination is Reality!*

Sources of Supply

The first question most asked when one completes reading this book is "Where can I buy these diverse *herbs?*"Because of the international content regarding the different products, a complete list is given for sources of supply. The list includes the United States, Canada, continental Europe, Asia, Africa, and the East. For herbs of the Orient, a list of Chinese companies is also given. Several firms listed are major wholesalers for those interested in cottage industries.

UNITED STATES

Aphrodesia Products, Inc.
45 Washington St.
Brooklyn, NY 11201

Green Mountain Herbs, Inc.
4890 Pearl St.
Boulder, CO 80301

Sweethardt Herbs
Box 12602
Austin, TX 78711

Hurov's Tropical Tree Nursery
Box 10387
Oahu, HI 96813

Wilcox Drug Co.
P.O. Box 391
Boone, NC 28607

S.B. Penick and Co.
100 Church St.
New York, NY 10007

Meer Corp.
9500 Railroad Ave.
North Bergen, NJ 07047

Nature's Way Products
P.O. Box 2233
Provo, UT 84601

Star and Crescent Herbs
8551 Thys Ct.,Suite C
Sacramento, CA 95828

The Whole Herb Co.
250 E. Blithedale
Mill Valley, CA 99494

San Francisco Herb, Tea & Spice
4543 Horton St.
Emeryville, CA 94608

China Herb Co.
1053 Tenth St.
San Diego, CA 92101

Magee Fur Co.
Eolia, MO 63344

Herbarium, Inc.
11016 152nd Ave.
Kenosha, WI 53140

Botanicals International, Inc.
2550 El Presidio St.
Long Beach, CA 90810

E.L. Scott & Co.
One World Trade Center, Suite 2347
New York, NY 10048

Schonfield & Sons, Inc.
12 White St.
New York, NY 10048

CANADA

Lifestream
12411 Vulcan Way
Richmond, B.C.
CANADA V6V 1J7

Botanical Health Products
P.O. Box 88, Station N
Montreal, Quebec, CANADA

Wide World of Herbs
11 St. Catherine St. E.
Montreal 129, CANADA

Golden Bough Herb Co.
212 MacKay Ave.
North Vancouver, B.C. CANADA

EUROPE

Louis-Henry Dossi
94 Avenue de Domont
95180 Montmorency
Paris, FRANCE

Wilhelm Kramer GmbH + Co.
8721 Schwebheim Ufr.
WEST GERMANY

Verenigde Nederlandse Kruidencooperative
V.N.K. Postbus 1
Elburg, HOLLAND

Heinrich Ambrosius
2000 Hamburg 13
Mittelwag 118
P.O. Box 2563 GERMANY

E.H. Worlee & Co.
Drogen Handelgesellschaft
200 Hamburg
39 Bellevue 7-8 GERMANY

Paul Muggenburg Drogen Huas
Wandaleneg 24
D-2000 Hamburg 1, WEST GERMANY

Donck
B-2620
Hemiksem (Antwerp), BELGIUM

Laboratories Galeniques Belges
7860 Lessines
BELGIUM

Occultique
73 Kettering Road
Northampton NN1 4AW

The Sorcerer's Apprentice
4/8 Burley Lodge Road
Leeds LS6 1QP

Medimpex
P.O. Box 126
Budapest, 5 HUNGARY

AFRICA

Ahmed Kamel
11, Talaat Harb Str
Cairo, EGYPT

Adel H. Azerfanous
5,/ ACT OR BASSILI STR
MAXAD ITA ALEX - EGYPT

EL-ADB
17 Kasr El-Nil St.
P.O. Box 2217
Cairo, EGYPT

CENTRAL & SOUTH AMERICA

Central de Drogas, S.A.
Dr. Liceaga No. 113
MEXICO 7, D.F.

Jose Asa
Morelos 110-90 Piso
MEXICO 6 D.F.

THE EAST

China National Native
82 Tung An Men St.
Peking, CHINA

Dr. Majithia
174 Samuel St.
Bombay, INDIA 9

Tsewi Corp.
2nd Fl. 67 Sung Chiang Road
P. O. Box #68-75
Taipei, Taiwan 104
REPUBLIC OF CHINA

Yoo Lee Imports & Export Co., Ltd.
P.O. Box Central 402
Seoul, KOREA

The Author

Richard Alan Miller is a scientist of extensive and multidimensional expertise. Receiving a degree in Theoretical Physics from Washington State University in 1966 he spent over a decade in biomedical research and development for some of the most prestigious and technologically sophisticated corporations in the United States including: The Boeing Company, The Strain Gage Research Laboratory and E.I. Dupont de Nemours Co. He worked for several years in the Department of Anesthesiology of the University of Washington incorporating his skills in both medicine and physics and has been published in several international journals for his work both in physics and parapsychology. He has taught parapsychology for credit in the Natural Sciences at several Universities and Colleges. He has also taught courses in shamanism, magick, and alchemy.

He is one of the "new" scientists recognizing that science should not and cannot be separated from the welfare of the human being. In 1973 he formed The Beltane Corporation specializing in the selling and study of herbs, spices and books focussing on herbs, health and the occult. This company was expanded into The Western Herb Farms, Inc. in 1980 to grow herbs, spices and botanicals. As a physicist he has invented several critical pieces of farm-machinery to assist the small-farm in harvest and processing. As an agricultural scientist he has developed specific farm-plans and crop sources to compete with currently imported spices and herbs. He is presently the founder and manager of The Methow Valley Herb Growers Association where he is continuing to research and employ the best of highly technical methods in a harmonious and non-injurious way.

The Artist

Elizabeth Gong has studied at the Cornish Institute for several years and has a degree in Graphic Design from the University of Washington. She is pursuing a career in graphics and illustration, specializing in technical and scientific illustration. She also paints in tempera and watercolor. She lives in Seattle with her husband and two children.

Chemistry

Absinthine — 66
Adrenergic — 84
Ajmaline — 83
Alcohol — 66, 78, 79, 80, 85, 89,
    101, 117
Alkaloid — 21, 74, 83, 85, 102,
    105, 113, 118, 123
Allyl Pyrocathecol — 24
Alpha Pyrones — 78
Aminezation — 70, 71
Ammonium Hydroxide — 101
Amphetamines — 89
Anabsinthin — 66
Analgesic — 60, 66
Anesthesia — 122
Anesthetic — 81, 122
Antihistamine — 89
Antispasmodic — 53
Antitoxin — 97
Aphrodesiac — 25, 41, 83
Arecoline — 24, 25
Aromatic — 74
Asarone — 70, 71
Asocrbic Acid — 85
Atrophine — 97, 122, 123, 124
Atrophine Sulfate — 122

B-asarone — 70
Baeocystin 109, 113
Banisterine — 104
Belladonna — 122

Bloodsugar — 34, 97
Bufotenin — 104

Cadinene — 24
Caffine — 32, 33, 34, 38, 41
Calcium Oxide — 24
Camphor — 29
Carbohydrates — 38
Carotid — 44
Cerebral Cortex — 38
Chanoclavine — 100
Chatinine — 54
Chavibetol — 24
Chavicol — 24
Cholinergic — 24, 84
CNS — 24, 38, 94, 95, 105
Cocaine — 33, 81
Codeine — 66
Coli Bacilli — 81
Cordial — 16

Decarboxylates — 95
Decongestant — 28
Depressant — 44, 105
Dextromethorphan Hydro-
    bromide — 66
Dihydrokawain — 78
Dihydromethysticin — 78
Dihydroyangonin — 78
D-isolysergic Acid Amide —
    100, 101

149

150

Geography/Tribes

France — 94
French Congo — 83

German — 91
Germany — 114
Goddess — 87, 88
God — 2, 31, 88
Gods — 86
Guardians — 80
Guatemala — 112

Hawaiian — 105
Herbarium of Apuleius — 65
Hindu — 23, 38, 69, 114
Hinduism — 103
Holy Guardian Angel — 74
Hopi Indian — 61

India — 23, 39, 73, 92, 93, 121, 122, 124
Indian — 32, 44, 45, 60
Indre — 94
Indus Valley — 92
Ipiklesis — 115

Jamaica — 37
Jamestown — 122
Japan — 27
John the Apostle — 94

Kamchadal — 92, 96
Koryak — 92, 96, 97

Laughing God — 87

Magickal Child — 116
Magyar — 91
Malay — 23
Malayan — 24
Malaysia — 73
Mapuche — 44
Masonic — 114, 117
Mayatecs — 100
Mazatecs — 112
Mexico — 15, 99, 113, 118, 121

Mexican — 99, 111, 117
Michoacau — 113
Middle East — 39
Mijes — 112
Minnesota — 69
Mixtecs — 112
Moola Bandha — 39, 41
Mooladahara-Chakra — 40
Moses — 71
Moso — 69

Nahoas — 113
Nahuatl — 100
New Guinea — 73, 74
New Zealand — 107
Non-Christian — 85
North America — 44, 60, 69, 91, 99
North Ashanti — 37
North Hemisphere — 53
Northern Indian — 61
Nova Scotia — 69

Oaxaca — 112, 118
Old Ones — 88
Ostyak — 92
Otomis — 113
Ox — 32
Ox-god — 2, 31

Pacific Coast — 92
Pagan — 85
Penobscot — 44
Philippines — 73
Philosopher's Stone — 117
Plaincourault — 94
Polynesia — 23, 77
Puebla — 113

Quaramis — 32

Rig Veda — 93

Samoans — 78
Sandwich Islands — 77

Botanics/Organics

Coconut oil — 79
Coffee — 25, 32, 33, 38
Cohoba — 104
Cola — 37
Colic root — 73
Conocybe — 118
Copal resin — 117
Copelandia — 118
Corn — 117
Cultivator's cap — 107

Dairy products — 89
Damiana — 15, 16, 17, 20, 45
Dandelion root — 48
Datora — 122
Datura — 122, 123, 124
Deadly nightshade — 123, 124
Desert tea — 27
Devil's apple — 121
Devil's eye — 124
Dhurstura — 122
D. Metal — 122

Elf's stool — 107
Ephedra — 27, 28, 29

Flying saucers — 99
Fly Agaric — 24, 91, 92, 94

Gabriel's trumpet — 121
Gagroot — 43
Galangal root — 73, 74
Galerina — 108
Gin — 85
Ginger — 64, 71, 74
Ginger beer — 74
Green ginger — 65
Guarana — 31, 32, 33, 34

Hawaiian wood rose seed — 105
Heavenly blue — 99
Henbane — 123, 124
Holy Basil — 124
Honey — 79, 96
Hood wort — 47

Iboga — 89
Indian snake root — 89
Indian tobacco — 43
India root — 73
Intoxicating pepper — 77
Iron — 48

Jamestown weed — 121
Jimson weed — 121, 122
Johimbe — 83

Kava Kava — 77, 78, 79, 80
Kola — 33
Kola nut — 37, 38, 41
Kowa — 77
Kowa Kowa — 77

La'aja shnash — 99
Lecithin — 79
Lettuce — 62
Lettuce opium — 59, 609, 61, 62
Liberty cap — 107
Licorice — 53
Lobelia — 17, 43, 45
Lopium — 59

Mad dogweed — 47
Madweed — 47
Magic mushroom — 107
Ma Huang — 28, 29
Mandrake — 123, 124
Maraba — 73
Marijuana — 19, 44, 48, 61, 79
Marjoram — 124
Mate — 33
May apple — 124
Meat — 117
Mexican damiana — 15
Mexican morning glory — 99
Milk — 96
Milkshake — 102
Mimosa — 104
Mint bidis — 25, 124
Monkshood — 124
Mormon tea — 27

Morning glory seed — 105
Mushroom — 92, 96, 112, 114,
    117, 118
Myrrh — 71

Naematoloma — 108
Narren Schwamm — 91
Niopo — 104
Nutmeg — 25, 105

Olive oil — 71
Omphalina — 108
Opium — 59, 60, 61
Oregon grape — 48

Panaeolus — 118
Panela supana — 31
Pank — 91
Pappaval — 124
Parica — 104
Parrot feathers — 117
Passion flower — 17, 19
Pausinystalia yohimba — 83
P. Baeocystis — 107, 108, 112,
    113, 118
P. Cubensis — 109
P. Cyanescens — 107, 109, 110
Pearly gates — 99
Pepper — 102
Peppermint — 20, 44, 56
Perfume — 74
Pernod — 66
Peyote — 102
Pholiotina — 118
Pinang — 23
Ping lang — 23
P. Mexicana — 111
Pong — 91
Pongo — 91
Popotillo — 27
P. Pelliculosa — 107, 110
P. Semilanceata — 107
Psilocybe mushroom — 88, 107
P. Strictipes — 107, 111

Racha — 69
Raindeer milk — 96
Raisin — 53
Rat root — 69
Rauwolfa — 89
Red clover — 48
Rum — 79

Saw palmetto berries — 16
Scullcap — 17, 20, 47, 48, 49,
    102
Shih-ch'ang pu — 69
Siri — 23
Soma — 91, 92, 93, 94, 96
Soot — 123
Sour orange — 124
Spaghetti — 114
Spearmint — 17, 56, 124
Squaw tea — 27
Stick tea — 27
Stinkweed — 121
Stromonium — 123
Strophana — 107
Stropharia — 118
Supari — 23
Swallow wort — 124
Sweet flag — 69
Sweet myrtle — 69
Sweet sedge — 69

Tatorach — 122
Tea — 33
Teamster's tea — 27
Thorn apple — 60, 124
Tiger balm — 29
Tlitlitzen — 99, 100
Tobacco — 23, 24, 44, 71, 99,
    117
Tobacco del diablo — 44
Tuba — 44
Tumeric — 25

Uabano — 31
Unimata — 122

Bibliography

Buckland R: *Practical Candle Burning*, Llewellyn Pub., St. Paul, MN, c 1972.

Church of The Tree of Life, *The First Book of Sacraments*, San Francisco, CA c 1972.

Crow WB: *The Occult Properties of Herbs*, Samuel Weiser, Inc., New York, NY c 1969.

Crowley A: *Liber Aleph*, Level Press, San Francisco, CA c 1974.

Crowley A: *Moonchild*, Samuel Weiser Inc, New York, NY c 1973.

Crowley A: *Magick: In Theory and Practice*, Castle Books, New York, NY c 1971.

Crowley A: *On Magick*, Level Press, San Francisco, CA c 1974.

Culling LT: *A Manual of Sex Magick*, Llewellyn Pub. St. Paul, MN c 1971.

Cutting WC: *Handbook of Pharmacology*, Meredith Corp, New York, NY c 1962.

Emboden W: *Narcotic Plants,* MacMillan Co, New York, NY c 1972.

Grieve M: *A Modern Herbal*, Dover Pub. New York, NY c 1971.

Grubber H: *Growing the Hallucinogens*, Level Press, San Francisco, CA c 1973.

Gottlieb A: *Encyclopedia of Sex Drugs and Aphrodisiacs*, Level Press, San Francisco, CA c 1974.

Hoffer A and Osmond H: *The Hallucinogens*, Academic Press, New York, NY c 1972.

Leary T, Metzner R and Alpert R: *The Psychedelic Experience*, University Books, New York, NY c 1972.

Leary T: *Neurologic*, Level Press, San Francisco, CA c 1973.

Meyer C: *The Herbalist*, De Vorss and Co., Marina Del Rey, CA c 1971.

Miller R. *Magickal Mushroom Handbook*, Homestead Press, Seattle, WA c 1976.

Monroe R: *Journies out of the Body*, De Vorss and Co, Marina Del Rey, CA c 1972.

Mumford J: *Sexual Occultism*, Llewellyn Pub., St. Paul, MN c 1975.

Pagan Way: *Pagan Rituals, Vol 1 and 2*, Earth Religion Supplies, New York, NY c 1975.

Powell E: *Tranquilization with Harmless Herbs*, Health Sciences Press, Sussex, England c 1965.

Regardie E: *The Tree of Life*, Samuel Weiser Inc, New York NY c 1969.

Riva A: *The Modern Herbal Spellbook*, International Imports, Toluca Lake CA c 1974.

Rose J: *Herbs and Things*, Grosset and Dunlap, New York, NY c 1972.

Schultes R and Hofmann A: *The Botany and Chemistry of Hallucinogens*, Charles Thomas Pub, Springfield, IL c 1973.

Shih-Chen L: *Chinese Medicinal Herbs*, Georgetown Press, San Francisco, CA c 1973.

Siegal R: "Herbal Intoxication," *JAMA*, Aug. 2, 1976, Vol 236, No. 5 p 473-476.

Steinmetz E: *Kava Kava*, Level Press, San Francisco, CA c 1973.

Superweed M: *Herbal Highs*, Stone Kingdom, San Francisco, CA c 1971.

Superweed M: *Aphrodisiacs*, Stone Kingdom, San Francisco, CA c 1971.

Twentieth Century Alchemist, *Legal Highs*, Level Press, San Francisco, CA c 1974.

U.S. Pharmacopoeia Convention, *The Pharmacopoeia of the USA*, P. Blakeston's Sons & Co., New York, NY c 1916.

Also by Richard Alan Miller,

the companion volume to
The Magical & Ritual Use of Herbs:

THE MAGICAL & RITUAL USE OF APHRODISIACS

Here, at last, is a comprehensive study of those "love foods" that truly enhance sexual experience. The author—a biochemist, physicist, and herbalist—brings to his book a thorough knowledge of the properties and specific effects of aphrodisiacs, as well as a deep appreciation for the psychological, spiritual, and ritual elements of human sexuality.

Invaluable information is provided on the chemistry, historical background, natural habitats, and correct identification and preparation of a wide range of aphrodisiacs. The author gives particular emphasis to the ritual use of each substance, drawing contemporary rituals from sources as diverse as tantric yoga and Western magic.

Special sections on hormones, foods, pharmaceuticals, and scents offer additional insight—both practical and magical—into the vast range and potential of sexual expression.

ISBN: 0-89281-062-9   *Quality Paperback*   *$8.95*